ISLAND ON EDGE

Pankaj Sekhsaria has worked on issues of the Andaman and Nicobar Islands for over three decades. He has authored/edited seven books on the islands, including *The Last Wave: An Island Novel, Waiting for Turtles, The Great Nicobar Betrayal* and now, *Island on Edge: The Great Nicobar Crisis.*

ISLAND ON EDGE

THE GREAT NICOBAR CRISIS

EDITED BY
PANKAJ SEKHSARIA

WESTLAND
NON·FICTION

WESTLAND
NON·FICTION

Published by Westland Non-Fiction, an imprint of Westland Books, a division of Nasadiya Technologies Private Limited, in 2025

No. 269/2B, First Floor, 'Irai Arul', Vimalraj Street, Nethaji Nagar, Alapakkam Main Road, Maduravoyal, Chennai 600095

Westland, the Westland logo, Westland Non-Fiction and the Westland Non-Fiction logo are the trademarks of Nasadiya Technologies Private Limited, or its affiliates.

Anthology copyright © Pankaj Sekhsaria, 2025

The copyright in the individual essays vests with the respective authors.

ISBN: 9789371978927

10 9 8 7 6 5 4 3 2 1

The views and opinions expressed in this work are the authors' own and the facts are as reported by them, and the publisher is in no way liable for the same.

All rights reserved

Typeset by Mukul

Printed at Thomson Press (India) Ltd

No part of this book may be reproduced, or stored in a retrieval system, or transmitted in any form or by any means, electronic, mechanical, photocopying, recording, or otherwise, without express written permission of the publisher.

Contents

About Great Nicobar Island	ix
Foreword by Vaishna Roy	xiii
Editor's Note: Closer to the Precipice	xvii

AN IMPERILLED FUTURE

1. An Island on Edge — 3
   PANKAJ SEKHSARIA
2. The Numbers Don't Add Up — 14
   M. RAJSHEKHAR
3. An Airport with Red Flags — 32
   SUMAN S.
4. What Do We Know About ANIIDCO? — 41
   PANKAJ SEKHSARIA AND RISHIKA PARDIKAR

INDIGENOUS LANDSCAPES

5. Tribal Lands Don't Show Up on Maps — 47
   RISHIKA PARDIKAR
6. Empower Earth's Guardians — 62
   AJAY SAINI AND MANISH CHANDI

7.	A Threat to Indigenous Languages Ajay Saini and Anvita Abbi	66
8.	A Violation of Laws, a Threat to Rights Pankaj Sekhsaria	71

TWO DECADES AFTER A TSUNAMI

9.	20 Christmases After the Tsunami Leesha K. Nair	79
10.	'The Death of Life' Ajay Saini	89

FRAGILE ECOLOGIES

11.	An Obit for Patai Takaru Rohan Arthur and T.R. Shankar Raman	99
12.	A Threat to Wildlife Saurav Harikumar	115
12A.	First Animal: Poems and Drawings Tansy Troy	125

EXPERT SPEAK

13.	Questioning Government Claims Rishika Pardikar	137
14.	A Can of Worms Vaishnavi Rathore	146
15.	Bolstering Security Without Ecological Harm	154

AFTERWORD

16. A Port of No Return   165
   PANKAJ SEKHSARIA

17. The Human Cost of Misgovernance   172
   M. RAJSHEKHAR

ANNEXURES

Annexure 1: Chronicle of an 'Ecocide' Foretold   193

Annexure 2: Letters Between Jairam Ramesh and
         Bhupender Yadav   199

Annexure 3: Press Release by Association of
         Indian Primatologists (AIP)   223

Annexure 4: Brief Project Timeline   229

Notes   233

About the Contributors   239

About Great Nicobar Island

Great Nicobar is the southernmost and fourth largest island in the Andaman and Nicobar archipelago. It is characterised by an undulating terrain and is the only island in Nicobar with perennial rivers—Galathea River being the largest. Located in the Indo-Malayan Biogeographic Zone, the island is covered with tropical evergreen forest, mixed evergreen forest, littoral forests and mangrove forest that are home to an abundant variety of rare and endemic faunal species.

The island is a part of the Sundaland Biodiversity Hotspot, one of the four hotspots in the country and was declared a UNESCO Biosphere Reserve in the year 2013. There are about 650 species of angiosperms, ferns, gymnosperms, bryophytes and lichens among others and over 1,800 species of fauna, with new species being discovered every year. The region also boasts of remarkable genetic biodiversity, exhibiting about 24 per cent endemism among some faunal groups. The island is bordered by fringing coral reefs throughout its 202 kilometres coastline, harbouring about 180 species of corals. Coupled with the sandy beaches along numerous bays, the island provides feeding and nesting ground for four species of marine sea turtles and together with Little Nicobar accounts for about 87 per cent of all turtle nesting across the Nicobar Islands. Great Nicobar falls under the East Australasian Bird Flyway and is categorized as an Endemic Bird Area and an Important Bird Area.

The entire island, except the seven revenue villages situated on the east coast, is protected as a Tribal Reserve meant for the two indigenous tribal communities—the Shompen and the Southern Nicobarese. The Shompen are a particularly vulnerable tribal group with a population of 229 as per the 2011 census and the Southern Nicobarese are a Scheduled Tribe with about 1,200 people. In late 1970s, about three hundred ex-servicemen families were settled on the island and today the settlers make up most of the population of the island, which is about 8,000.

About Great Nicobar Island

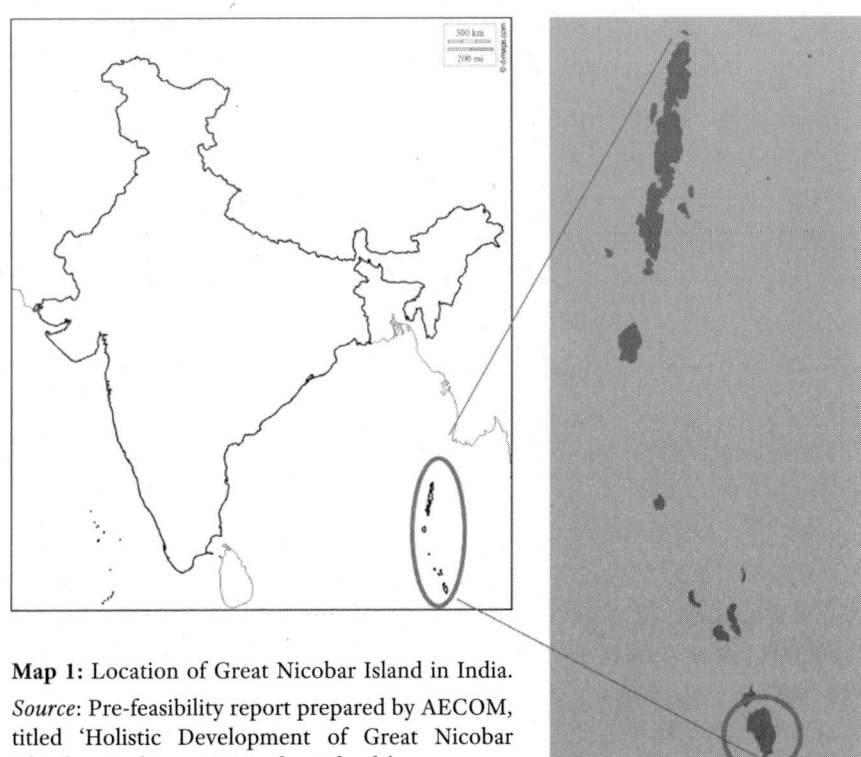

Map 1: Location of Great Nicobar Island in India.

Source: Pre-feasibility report prepared by AECOM, titled 'Holistic Development of Great Nicobar Island at Andaman & Nicobar Islands'

Foreword

A recent piece in *The Hindu* reports that the Environment Impact Assessment study carried out for the Great Nicobar project significantly downplays the risk of future earthquakes. The geoscientist, C.P. Rajendran, told the newspaper that the Great Nicobar Island was an 'extremely geo-dynamic area and major infrastructure projects here are particularly vulnerable. It is better to avoid such an area for a port or a container terminal'.

In 2023, when *Frontline* did its first cover story on the mega infrastructure project planned for this remote island, three disaster specialists from the School of Disaster Studies, Tata Institute of Social Sciences, Mumbai—Janki Andharia, V. Ramesh and Ravinder Dhiman—wrote that they had written to the government pointing out that a simple analysis of seismic activity showed that the proposed container terminal 'would be located at a site that experiences about 44 earthquakes every year'.

When seismic risk evaluations—which experts say have not even been undertaken at the Great Nicobar project site—show a very high probability of earthquakes, most countries do not allow megaprojects at such sites. The project proponent in Great

Nicobar, however, told the writers mentioned earlier that the structures would be made earthquake-proof and a detailed disaster management plan would be put in place. In other words, instead of preventing a tragedy, the government prefers a post-catastrophe response—to a mammoth project whose initial budget was Rs 72,000 crore, later raised to Rs 82,000 crore even before the first stone was laid.

But earthquakes are hardly the only danger. The Great Nicobar Infrastructure Project is veiled by a deep opacity, with access denied to vital documents and reports on the pretext that it is a defence undertaking that demands secrecy. Yet, on the cards are a transshipment port, international airport, township and power plant—none of which are defence projects. And all of which are planned on a scale that is entirely too great for the island of Great Nicobar. Take this number alone: the projected population for 2025 for the entire Andaman and Nicobar Islands is 4,05,000. Great Nicobar, which is a 920 square kilometres island in the archipelago, has a population of about 8,000. The project envisages that upon completion, some 3,50,000 people will settle on Great Nicobar alone. This is not development, it is unalloyed disaster.

On the path to this disaster lie various other cavalier depredations—such as the clearing of at least 130 square kilometres of pristine tropical evergreen rainforest. While the government has admitted this entails the cutting down of nearly a million trees, ecologists say the number could be ten times as much. At a time of great climate change, what sort of policy myopia would make India want to get rid of this immense rainforest carbon sink?

And what degree of plutomania would countenance tree-felling and concrete jungles, mega ports and settlements on a designated tribal reserve that is also a UNESCO-designated global biosphere reserve? Galathea Bay Wildlife Sanctuary, notified in 1997 for monitoring marine turtles, was de-notified with vulgar haste in

2021 by the National Board for Wildlife, which turned its back on the Giant leatherback and other species the sanctuary protected.

The island is, in fact, rich with endemic wildlife; the Nicobar megapode, Nicobar tree shrew, Nicobar sparrowhawk and Nicobar macaque, to name a few. The Association of Indian Primatologists has said that the project could result in the functional extinction of the Nicobar macaque. 'The project proponents are indifferent toward the fragile ecosystems of the island and have not prioritised its unique biodiversity in their decisions', a spokesperson told *Frontline*.

Besides, UNESCO mentions 650 species of flora on the biosphere, including angiosperms, ferns, bryophytes, screwpine and mangrove varieties, many of them endemic to the island. In fact, one of the charges levelled by ecologists against the Environmental Impact Assessment is that it has underreported the extent of coral reefs and biodiversity on the island to downplay the impact of the project.

Frontline, the fortnightly magazine that I edit, published two cover stories in the space of roughly two years, with around a dozen essays by experts that examined the extent of the environmental carnage being considered on the island. We also published a compilation of articles, titled *The Great Nicobar Betrayal,* which was curated by Pankaj Sekhsaria, whose life's work has been on the Andaman and Nicobar Islands and who has been fighting against this project tirelessly.

On 10 October 2023, the National Green Tribunal constituted a high-powered committee to re-examine the environmental clearance granted to the project, and one awaits the report with anxiety. There are also multiple interventions in the Calcutta High Court. In fact, the legal legerdemain at play is another story waiting to be written.

But let us not forget the other hapless victims of this Tughlaqian undertaking: the indigenous population of Great Nicobar. The island with its ancient forests and beaches is the ancestral home of the Shompen, a particularly vulnerable tribal group, and the Nicobarese, a scheduled tribe, who have lived here for millennia. Writing in *Frontline,* the anthropologist Ajay Saini spoke of his encounters with these people. 'What is a forest to the people who call it home? My ethnographic research in the Nicobar has revealed the profound spiritual connection its indigenous inhabitants share with their lands, forests, and ocean. To them, the forest is more than just trees. It is the foundation of their identity, a sacred sanctuary, above all, it is family.'

Can we as Indians, who vaunt our spirituality, understand the spiritual nature of this bond? Can we understand that a massive concrete project on a tribal reserve is like a bulldozer smashing our homes? Or have we become so enamoured with bulldozers that we will let the lives and homes of these vulnerable Shompen and Nicobarese be casually destroyed because we want another port, another colony, another airport?

These are the questions we must ask. Not just in Great Nicobar, but in the many forests and biospheres of India where corporate greed is playing out with untrammelled ease.

Island on Edge is an important sequel to *Frontline*'s first volume, and adds data, details and updates that take forward our understanding of the damage that threatens Great Nicobar, and one hopes it will inspire ordinary citizens to ask the right questions now.

Vaishna Roy
Editor, *Frontline*

Editor's Note:
Closer to the Precipice

It is little more than a year since we published *The Great Nicobar Betrayal*, a quick collection of some sharp writing that offered easy but wide-ranging engagement with the disaster being planned for the island of Great Nicobar.

The book received an enthusiastic response even as it was tinged with obvious concern: 'the slim and punchy little book (...) augurs a coming death,' T.R. Shankar Raman wrote worryingly in his review for *Mongabay* (Annexure 1). 'The portentous subtitle, "Pushing a Vulnerable Island Knowingly into Disaster",' he noted further, 'foreshadows the impending tragedy of its developmental death.' Ram Guha, writing in *The Telegraph*, highlighted the gap filled by this collection that the 'national media' has left pretty much unaddressed, while for Lakshmi Ravinder Nair, writing in the *Journal of Threatened Taxa*, the book worked 'like an out-of-breath town crier arriving in the crowded places of our minds and city spaces to inform us of the happenings in our beloved archipelago.'

This 'out-of-breath' crying appears, importantly and also gratifyingly, to have reached out widely across the country and beyond, facilitating conversations, raising questions and evoking expressions of even more concern. We've managed to get the volume translated into two languages as well—the Bengali version *Great Nicobar Prakalpa: O Kicchu Prashna* was released in Kolkata in March, and the Hindi edition titled *Great Nicobar: Kahani Vishwasghat Ki* that was released a couple of months later. One had not imagined that this collection would evoke such a response, just as one did not anticipate there would be the need and indeed the material to do a second volume in such quick time. There are two things that need to be said about this.

First, the deep concerns and extensive questioning in the media, in Parliament and increasingly by the scientific community notwithstanding, there is absolutely no rethinking on the project. The massive Myanmar earthquake of March 2025 and the devastation that has followed in its wake (3,000 people dead and counting) could—and should—serve as a wake-up call, but there are no signs of that. The islands themselves have continued to experience earthquakes on a regular basis (once a week on average) and recent scientific work has thrown even more light on the vulnerability of these islands in the context of the tsunamigenic earthquake of December 2004.[1] It is baffling that we continue to ignore such clear and precise scientific warnings, and this highlights the need to ensure the spotlight is not shifted from the project.

Second, it is the continued research on the project that has prompted and facilitated this follow-up volume. This, along with extensive writing in the media, has been uncovering layers and layers of information and even more deceit, compromise and contradiction. There is a question and a problem one can see at every step and in every aspect of the project, and the manner in which it is being pushed.

Frontline has again taken a lead with continous coverage and a second special cover package, titled 'A Fragile Future', which was published in March 2025. This cover package is indeed one of the key catalysts for this edited volume just like the first special cover package, titled 'Nicobar Nightmare', published in January 2023, along with *Sanctuary Asia*'s Great Nicobar special issue of April 2023 was the trigger for Volume 1.[2]

The four stories in *Frontline*'s March 2025 issue are at the heart of this volume, and I am deeply grateful to Vaishna Roy, editor of *Frontline*, for her wholehearted support. Special thanks also the contributors to this issue: M. Rajshekhar for an excellent ground report combined with what is undoubtedly the first critically in-depth analysis of the shaky economic and financial foundations of the entire project; T.R. Shankar Raman and Rohan Arthur, two of India's leading ecologists, for their piece that is as scientifically rigorous as it is deeply philosophical; and Saurav Harikumar who has put together a small but vital snapshot of ten rare and unique creatures we find on Great Nicobar and in the surrounding waters. A big thanks to Tansy Troy as well for her beautifully evocative drawings and poems on the rare and the endangered of Great Nicobar.

The volume also includes a lot of other writing: incisive pieces that open up new areas of investigation, a set of expert interviews that provide important new insights and a bunch of editorial pieces I have written myself that seek to further uncover the innumerable contradictions and betrayals.

We wrap up the volume with a larger and detailed piece, again by M. Rajshekhar, that looks at the larger contemporary context of these islands within which the Great Nicobar project has to be and should be located. Like last time, we also have a lot of other complementary information, including tables and boxes, a timeline for the project, and annexures with important and interesting developments.

I am deeply grateful to all the authors: Rishika Pardikar, Manish Chandi, Ajay Saini, Anvita Abbi, Vaishnavi Rathore, Umesh Anand and Leesha Nair, in addition to those already mentioned earlier. Deep gratitude also to the publications—*Frontline*, *The Hindu*, *Indian Express*, *Hindustan Times*, *Civil Society*, *Earth Island Journal*, *Article 14*, *Scroll.in*, *The Diplomat*, *The Wire* and *The News Minute*— for allowing me to include their contributions in this volume.

I would also like to thank Karthika V.K., Sonia Madan, Vedika, Shatrughan Pandey and Mukul at Westland for agreeing to do this volume and ensuring its publication within a rather short time frame.

It is increasingly clear now that this project is going to be an unmitigated disaster, and the least we can do is ensure we all know the how, why and what of it. Note, for instance, that the cost of the project has escalated by nearly 15 per cent from Rs 72,000 crore to Rs 81,000 crore in just three years.[3] It is certain this will only increase, and is another indication that the project proponents and investors have no idea of what they are getting into.

This indeed is the primary purpose of putting together what we might call *The Great Nicobar Betrayals*—plural for the two volumes, but more significantly for the many continued betrayals of an island far away from the vision and the consciousness of the country, its people and importantly, those who are making decisions about it.

Pankaj Sekhsaria

AN IMPERILLED FUTURE

1

An Island on Edge

PANKAJ SEKHSARIA

A series of developments and new information that has come to light in recent months have raised further questions about the planned Rs 80,000+ crore mega infrastructure project on Great Nicobar Island (GNI). The NITI Aayog–piloted initiative has four components: a transshipment terminal in Galathea Bay, an airport, a greenfield township and tourism project, and a gas-powered power plant

One of the sources of new information is the minutes of a meeting held in Port Blair on 4 October 2024, under the chairmanship of the Managing Director of the Andaman and Nicobar Islands Integrated Development Corporation Ltd (ANIIDCO), the project proponent. The other is a series of letters exchanged since April 2024 between the Ministry of Ports, Shipping and Waterways (MoPSW), the Ministry of Home Affairs (MHA), and the andaman and nicobar administration.

Those who attended the 4 October meeting included senior officials of ANIIDCO, including its Managing Director and its General Manager; representatives of various departments of the Andaman and Nicobar Administration such as environment and forests, the public works division, the port management board and the tribal welfare department; and representatives of Egis India Consulting Engineers Pvt. Ltd, a Gurugram-based consulting firm tasked with preparing the detailed master plan for the trunk infrastructure and township.[1]

Forest Destruction

This component alone covers a massive 130 square kilometres of largely primary tropical rainforest of the total project area of a little over 160 square kilometres.

A key concern with the project from the very beginning has been the scale of forest destruction proposed, with a large portion allocated for the township that Egis is now planning. Initial numbers for trees to be cut ranged from 8.65 lakh, as mentioned in the March 2021 project proposal prepared by AECOM India Ltd,[2] to 9.64 lakh, stated by the government in Parliament in August 2023. This gained further traction when, in August 2024, ANIIDCO invited expressions of interest for 'enumeration, felling, logging and transportation of these trees'.[3] This indicated, first and foremost, that the project proponent did not actually know the number of trees to be cut.

Recent media reports based on calculations done by scientists suggested that the 8.65 lakh number, staggering as it was, has been underestimated by at least a factor of three; most likely even more. One estimate suggested the trees standing in these 130 square kilometres of forests could be as many as 10 million. This alone vitiates the forest and environment clearances granted by the Ministry of Environment, Forest and Climate Change (MoEFCC) in 2022—both because they were based on incomplete and inaccurate information, and due to the underestimation of the environmental impact and biodiversity loss.

The minutes of the 4 October meeting add many more dangerously comical twists to this story. It suggests, for instance, that various project-implementing agencies explore 'the possibility of utilising the soft woods [cut from these forests] as biomass for power generation' and that the confirmation for the same 'be obtained within one week'.[4]

The forests of Great Nicobar are an unexplored biodiversity treasure trove besides being the traditional home to communities such as the Shompen, whose survival is intricately linked to these forests and who have special status under Indian law. Suggesting that millions of these trees be burned for power generation is akin to someone entering a library and lighting up rare manuscripts for the evening barbecue, or bulldozing an ancient temple and crushing the stones for their use in road construction. The idea of a wood-fired power plant, bizarre as it might sound in today's era, is not even part of the proposal.

Equally intriguing in the minutes of the same meeting is the list of agencies that have shown interest in enumerating, felling and disposing of the trees in response to ANIIDCO's call. It includes Konkan Railway Corporation Ltd, RITES, MECON, EQMS Global, FALCON Resilient Infra, Ultra Tech and Terracon India. Even a cursory look at their primary missions and visions shows that tree-felling operations are not part of their scheme of things and that they have no related experience or expertise.

It has become a case of anything goes. Indeed, if a company like ANIIDCO—that has only sold liquor, milk and petroleum for more than three decades—can be entrusted with a Rs 80,000 crore infrastructure project in one of the world's most difficult landscapes, entities that build railways and ports or sell consultancy services could also do anything, including counting trees, cutting them and burning the timber for power generation.

Logging Lessons from History

It is little realised, however, that tree-felling and transporting timber in these islands have a difficult and complex history—not just in terms of tribal rights and biodiversity destruction but from a logistics point of view as well. Logging here goes back more than a century when it was started in the early 1900s by the British. Clear-felling of the kind now proposed in Great Nicobar was stopped in the islands many decades ago. Importantly, large-scale felling for commercial purposes ever happened only in the Andaman Islands; commercial and large-scale tree-felling was never allowed in the Nicobars.

A look at the records of timber felled in the islands provides additional insight. The average extraction of timber in the islands (Andamans) from the late 1960s to about 2000, when logging was drastically curtailed, was about 1.2 lakh cubic metres a year (see Table 1). Even if one assumes that an average rainforest tree has about 3 cubic metres of timber, this amounts to cutting of 40,000 trees a year. And if one goes by the project proponent's original but grossly underestimated number of 8.65 lakh, it still means that it will take two decades of continuous logging to clear these forests.

Logging in a forest also needs tremendous skill besides infrastructure such as heavy machinery and perhaps elephants as well. Getting it all in place will be a task in itself, and the basic numbers suggest that this is simply not possible within the period envisioned for this project. This would be an extremely difficult ask even in the Andaman Islands, which has a history of logging and the basic infrastructure for the same. To create this in Great Nicobar will be doubly difficult and raises serious questions about the timelines, project execution and the project's basic financial viability.

Nothing highlights the complications better than the interlinked issues of compensatory afforestation. In what is one of the most absurd and farcical cases of compensatory afforestation

Table 1. Timber Extraction, Andaman Islands, 1968–2004

Year	Quantity (cu. m)	Year	Quantity (cu. m)
1968–83 (annual average)	118,800	1991–92	105,319
		1992–93	125,670
1980–81	165,726	1993–94	130,136
1981–82	162,241	1994–95	135,523
1982–83	147,308	1995–96	126,579
1983–84	147,309	1996–97	107,443
1984–85	132,579	1997–98	77,097
1985–86	145,305	1998–99	62,623
1986–87	131,888	1999–2000	47,617
1987–88	115,801	2000–01	40,053
1988–89	123,678	2001–02	4,711
1989–90	117,746	2002–03	Nil
1990–91	103,660	2003–04	Nil

Source: Pankaj Sekhsaria and Vishvajit Pandya, *The Jarawa Tribal Reserve Dossier: Cultural and Biological Diversity in the Andaman Islands*, Paris: UNESCO; Pune: Kalpavriksh, 2010, p. 46.

ever, the diversion of 130 square kilometres of pristine tropical forest in Great Nicobar is being compensated for by declaring 260 square kilometres of land in Haryana and Madhya Pradesh as forest land. Under this swap, in August 2024, the government notified 243.5 square kilometres of land in the Aravallis in Haryana as protected forest.

In what is a double whammy, however, 119.5 acres (48.36 hectares) of this very forest land was handed over almost immediately by Haryana's mining department to a private entity for stone quarrying. This is a serious illegality whichever way one might choose to look at it.

Legal Issues

There are also serious legal issues that emanate from the 2002 report of the Supreme Court–appointed Shekhar Singh Commission and the court's orders based on it. While the project proponent says in multiple places that the tree-felling will be done in accordance with the Supreme Court orders and the Shekhar Singh report, it fails to note at least two key points of the Supreme Court order:

a) 'All felling of trees ... in national parks, sanctuaries, the tribal reserves and all other areas shall stand suspended'; and
b) '... there should first be compulsory afforestation/regeneration [and] the felling permissions would be based upon the extent of regeneration of forest undertaken and not the other way round.'

To now suggest that such massive tree-felling will take place in such a short time with no evidence of any afforestation or regeneration, and that the timber will be burned in power plants, leave alone the fact that part of land in Haryana has been handed over for quarrying, is a serious violation of the Supreme Court orders.

Planned Projects and Security Concerns

New information, which has now become available in the letters exchanged between the MoPSW and the Andaman and Nicobar Administration, raises additional questions of the initial planning, the cost estimates and violation of due process. The ministry has now proposed a host of new projects, including an international cruise terminal to facilitate a 'global port-led city' and accommodate high-end tourists, a ship-building and ship-repair facility, and an export-import (exim) port to help bring in construction material from neighbouring countries.

First, in April 2024, Rajiv Kumar, Under-Secretary in the ministry (Sagarmala III), wrote to the Chief Secretary of the Andaman and Nicobar Administration asking for 100 acres of land with 500 metres seafront for ship-repair and ship-building facilities in Campbell Bay, the administrative headquarters of GNI.

This was followed by another request in May for details that would enable Campbell Bay to be declared an exim port for importing construction materials. Then Shipping Secretary, T.K. Ramachandran, himself wrote to the Secretary, MHA, in September, advocating for an international and domestic cruise terminal as part of the project 'to accommodate high-end and domestic tourists'.

Not only are these not part of the original proposal, they might not even be permissible under the law. The Andaman and Nicobar Administration and ANIIDCO have responded, arguing that ship-repair will not be compatible with the purpose of the greenfield township and it 'could undermine the envisioned water front activities particularly the tourism infrastructure envisaged for GNI'.

It was also noted that the coastline came under the coastal regulation zone (CRZ 1a) as it has coral reefs along almost the entire east coast, and that this would be a constraint for ship-repair activity as well.

Denial of Information

What is also striking to note in this context is the position of the MHA and the consistent denial of any information by the MoEFCC. In November 2022, Prasad Kale, a Mumbai-based researcher, filed an RTI application seeking a range of information from the MoEFCC related to the forest and environment clearances granted to the project. But the MoEFCC refused to divulge the information, invoking issues of sovereignty, integrity, security and strategic concerns of the country via Section 8(1)(a) of the RTI Act.

It also cited a submission made by the MHA (DO letter No. 15020/24/2020-Plg. Cell dated 15 September 2022) noting that the airport was a military–civil, dual-use airport and is supposed to be under the operational control of the Navy. This was also upheld by the Central Information Commission through its order of 28 June 2024, except for the directive to provide information on the compensatory afforestation proposed for the project.

Researchers have pointed to the incongruence of denying information on the entire project when only one component—the airport—had a defence connection.

The proposals of the Ministry of Ports, Shipping and Waterways also suggest that it is neither aware of the strategic concerns that have been used to deny information nor the fact that many of these activities, such as ship-building, a cruise terminal and high-end international tourism, are themselves contrary to this strategic purpose. This is in addition to the impact that these new projects will have on the environment, the need for additional environmental clearances and the possible cost implications.

Cost Escalation

Considerable cost escalation is already being seen even without these new additions. This is most evident, for instance, in case of the transshipment port, which is at the heart of the entire project. The estimated cost of the port has already gone up from Rs 35,959 crore as mentioned in the project proposal in March 2021 to Rs 43,796 crore in the September 2024 letter written by the Joint Secretary of MoPSW to the Andaman and Nicobar Administration. This is already a 20 per cent escalation in less than three years, and no work has even begun on the ground.

A perusal of the history of this project, through articles published regularly in *Frontline* as well as in the recently curated *The Great Nicobar Betrayal*, shows a casualness, apathy and lack of rigour—

whether in the quality of the environmental impact assessment process, concern for the rights of indigenous communities, the geological vulnerability of the place, or the cost escalations and their implications.

One striking example of this casualness and lack of rigour is the change in the position of key players involved in the project. One is AECOM India Ltd, the Gurugram-based consultant whose March 2021 pre-feasibility report laid out the contours of the project. This report gave a very positive evaluation of the economic and other benefits of the transshipment port at Galathea Bay, and was the basis for the approval of the entire project.

For instance, the executive summary of the report notes: 'The proposed port will allow Great Nicobar to participate in the regional and global maritime economy by becoming a major player in cargo transshipment.' It notes further that the locational advantage of being on international sea route will allow Great Nicobar to be 'a sustainable, green, global destination for business, trade, and leisure'.

The same AECOM had a diametrically opposite view of the entire Andaman and Nicobar Islands just five years earlier, in 2016. In its 'Final Report for Sagarmala' prepared for the MoPSW and the Indian Ports Association, AECOM, along with its consultant partner McKinsey, was categorical that no site in the Andaman and Nicobar Islands, including Great Nicobar, was good enough for a transshipment port. Its detailed technical note concluded the following, after evaluating many options:

> Development of FTWZ [free trade and warehousing zone] and transshipment hub may not be a favourable option due to the insufficient hinterland demand and supply.... Bunkering is also a non-starter ... as Great Nicobar does not have any refining capacity of its own. Setting up of cruise facilities is the only feasible option that look promising at

these islands as it will require minimal infrastructure and the exotic locations combined with many water-related activities makes it a favourite tourism destination.

Intriguingly, there has been no explanation anywhere for this drastic change in stand, and how a site that was completely inappropriate for a port and related facilities in 2016 suddenly became the most suited and viable for the same a mere five years later.

Changing Stands

Equally, if not more, striking is the change in the position of Deepak Apte, a Mumbai-based marine biologist, who as chair of the MoEFCC's expert appraisal committee, helmed the environmental and CRZ clearance for the project. He not only steered the clearance process within fifteen months but also overlooked several key concerns.

These included the fact that the project proponent, ANIIDCO, has experience only in selling milk, liquor and petroleum products; the shockingly poor quality of the environmental impact assessment report; the scientifically and ecologically unsound proposal for compensatory afforestation in Haryana; the failure to confirm the actual number of trees to be cut; the decision to hold a public hearing in January 2022 at the height of the COVID-19 pandemic; and his role in heading a committee that laid down unscientific and unimplementable environmental conditions.

Just three years earlier, Apte had held a diametrically opposite position on the development projects for these islands in general and Great Nicobar in particular. As the incumbent director of the Bombay Natural History Society, Apte had penned a scathing editorial titled 'Nicobar and Lakshadweep in Peril' in the July–September 2018 issue of *Hornbill*, the society's publication for its members.[5] He wrote,

The magnitude of infrastructural development envisaged for these (Andaman and Nicobar) Islands is not just scary but incomprehensible by any means.... If one browses through the recent documents of NITI Aayog 'Incredible Islands of India (Holistic Development)' one would be bewildered by the changes that are slated to take place in these extremely fragile ecosystems.... The most worrying project proposed is the trans-shipment project at Great Nicobar. The proposed site abuts Galathea Beach which is one of the best known nesting sites for Leatherback Turtle....

While our mainland coastline has undergone tremendous transformation, developments now taking place along the most pristine seascapes of Andaman & Nicobar and Lakshadweep will spell doom for these last remaining global marine biodiversity hotspots.... We hope wisdom will prevail and areas like Suheli, Little Andaman, Great Nicobar, Little Nicobar, Narcondam Island, and Interview Island will remain protected for their biodiversity and intrinsic ecological values as national assets and for the future prosperity of the nation.

There is no evidence that anything changed in the material reality of these islands, their value, beauty or vulnerability between 2018, when this editorial was written, and November 2022, when the very same project was granted all clearances by a committee he headed.

On the shifting sands of the coastline of Great Nicobar, these changing stands are killing one of the most valuable, precious and irreplaceable treasures of this planet. No questions asked, no accountability demanded.

(First published in *Frontline*, 3 March 2025.)

2

The Numbers Don't Add Up

M. Rajshekhar

On the ground in Campbell Bay, the government's promise to remake Great Nicobar into the Indian equivalent of Singapore, Hong Kong or Macau is starting to feel imminent. Not only has a steady stream of Central Government bureaucrats and ministers been flocking to Great Nicobar, at least two firms have begun preparatory work on the project, which involves building a transshipment terminal and a township to support it on the island.

In the last one year alone, the Prime Minister's Principal Secretary, P.K. Mishra; the Home Secretary, Ajay Bhalla; the Union Minister for Shipping, Sarbananda Sonowal; and the Union Minister of State for Ports, Shipping and Waterways, Shantanu Thakur, have toured the island. In late January 2025, senior bureaucrats from the Ministry of Home Affairs and the National Thermal Power Corporation Limited (NTPC) also paid a visit. The Port Blair–based SS Associates is soil-testing for Egis India, a Gurgaon-based engineering consultancy that bagged the bid to design the township. Another company, owned by local panchayat pramukh (head), E.S. Rajesh, is setting up boundary pillars in revenue areas, marking locations for each project component.

There are other signs of change as well. A turtle hatchery on the eastern flank of Galathea Bay has been removed. Locals see more vehicle movement than before. They also say land prices in Great Nicobar are rising fast. 'The price used to be around Rs 4 lakh an acre and has now climbed to Rs 45 lakh,' said Sanjay Singh, a civil contractor in Campbell Bay who is also a local BJP leader.

In a few weeks, the activity will accelerate. In September 2024, even before the project's Stage 2 forest clearance came in, the Andaman and Nicobar Industrial Development Corporation (ANIIDCO) had invited expression of interest for logging. Even though a staggering 1 million trees (as per official estimates; scientific estimates run higher) will be cut, the Stage 2 clearance is expected soon. Thereafter, once ANIIDCO chooses from the thirteen firms that participated in the tender, 130 square kilometres of forest will be clear-felled.

In the meantime, the island is seeing a clampdown. Fearing negative publicity—given the project's implications for the island's endemic biodiversity, species like the leatherback turtle that nests in Galathea Bay, ancient forests and indigenous communities—the Union Territory's (UT) administration is trying to keep visitors out. Unlike the rest of the island, Campbell Bay is revenue land and, ergo, open to all Indians. Yet, as this reporter personally found, the administration is telling visitors—even tourists—to get approvals from Campbell Bay's Assistant Commissioner (AC) before it issues flight tickets. Thereafter, the AC's office doesn't respond to email and WhatsApp requests.

'I did my last tour there in March 2023,' a Port Blair–based birding tour operator told *Frontline* on condition of anonymity.

'After that, no more tours. In April 2023, they issued an informal order that tourists cannot visit Campbell Bay even though they have no authority to bar visitors.'

A reporting team from the online news organisation *The News Minute* that reached the island—making the thirty-hour journey by ship—told *Frontline* about the struggle to get access to the forests and about being followed and questioned by local police and Intelligence Bureau officers. The police even tried to stop the two journalists from interviewing local Nicobarese people.

Both haste and secrecy are instrumental choices; despite major concerns ranging from the project's ecological and social fallouts to its weak economic foundations, they help the government present a fait accompli on the ground.

———•———

At present, feeder ships carry as much as two-thirds of all container cargo from India to Colombo, Port Klang (Malaysia) or Singapore where they are loaded onto larger vessels. India's Ministry of Shipping, therefore, believes that a transshipment port at Galathea Bay will not only save as much as $200 million to $220 million (Rs 17,000 crore to Rs 18,700 crore) each year in foreign exchange, it will also help India participate in the regional and global maritime economy and make it a major player in cargo transshipment.

And yet, given its scale and distance from the mainland, the Great Nicobar project will be expensive. 'The cost of construction in the islands cannot be compared with that in the mainland,' said the head of a civil construction firm in Port Blair on condition of anonymity. 'Here, everything costs 2.5–3 times more.'

At the same time, Great Nicobar cannot charge more for cargo movement than rival ports like Colombo. Given that the prevailing market rate is about $35 per container, even if the project handles the targeted 4 million containers, the revenue won't cover even interest payments, as this article will show.

Private bidders, therefore, want the government to pay for the port construction. As for the township, ports need towns to provide the services that shippers will require. As a Mumbai-based maritime consultant said, 'Great Nicobar is not competing with just Singapore or Colombo's ports but the cities around them too.' However, unlike regular ports that have a large hinterland producing goods and services, transshipment ports produce very little economic activity. 'The economic value captured by a container is as much as $25,000–$30,000,' said the consultant. 'The economic activity produced by a transshipment port, in contrast, is miniscule. All you are doing is unloading one container, putting it on a berth, then loading it onto another ship.'

In the absence of strong revenues from the port to recover investments on the township, the government is trying to create fresh business models for the city—a tourism hub, a shipbuilding yard, a ship-repair yard, a terminal for cruise ships and so on. These plans too, however, will face higher construction costs and equivalent concerns about competitiveness. Compounding matters, some of these additions might work at cross-purposes—like an airport for 2 million passengers and the plan for a defence base, the latter to ensure that the islands aren't annexed and also for India to gain leverage over China, which depends on the Malacca shipping route.

If neither the city nor the port can pay for itself, the government might have to provide viability gap funding. In that case, its outlay on the project, which has already climbed from Rs 10,000 crore (2020) to Rs 72,000 crore (2022) and again to Rs 81,000 crore (2024), will rise yet higher.

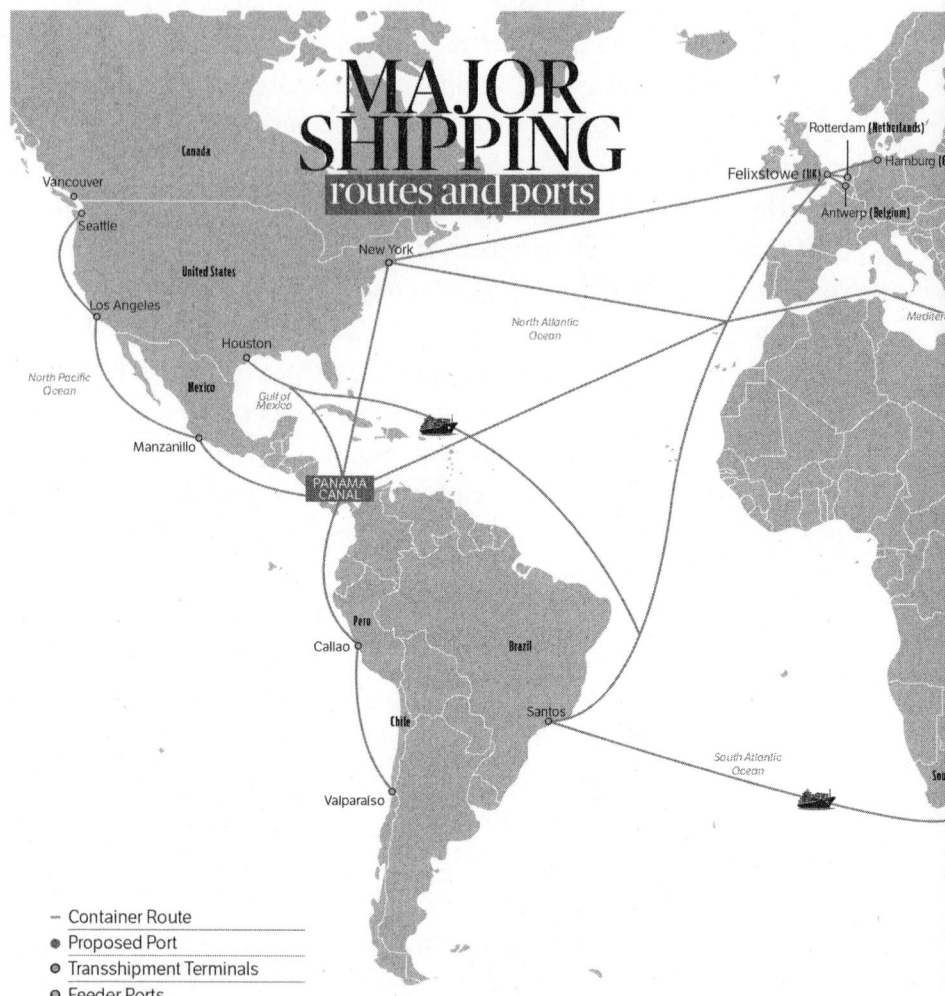

Map 2: Major shipping routes and ports.
Source: *Frontline* | © 2025 The Hindu Group

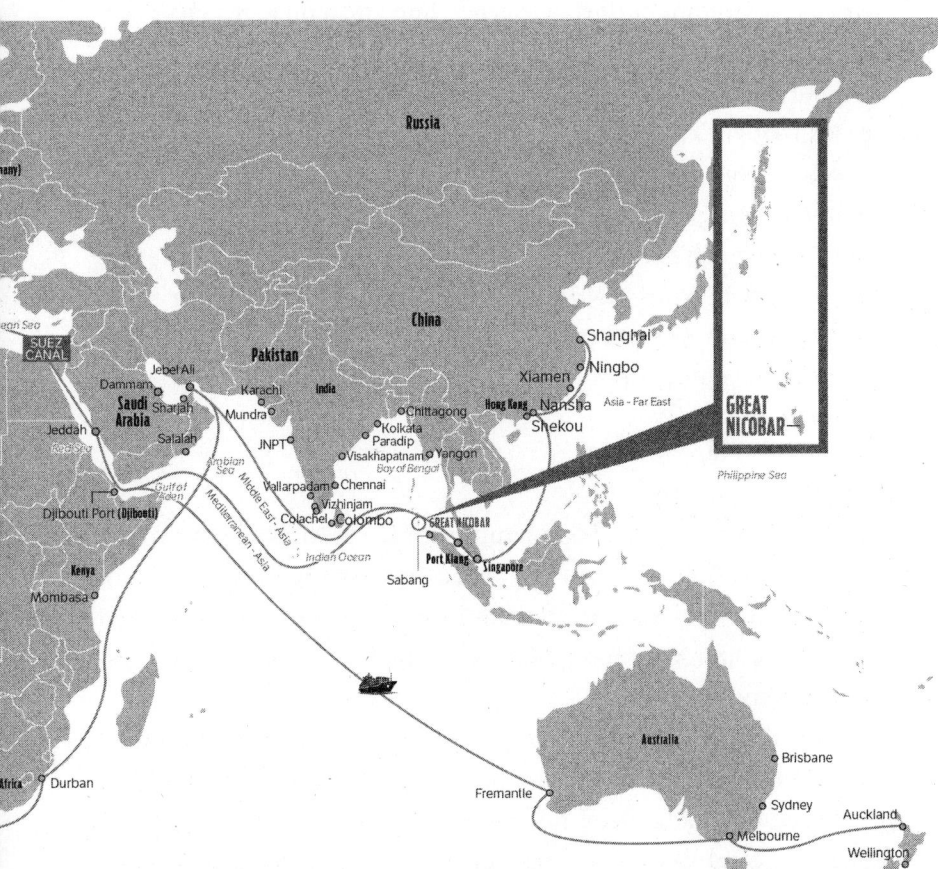

Ships coming from the west with cargo for India's eastern seaboard can drop their cargo at Great Nicobar instead of Colombo. Similarly, ships coming from the east can leave their containers at Great Nicobar instead of Colombo, Port Klang, or Singapore. There is nuance here. A large east-bound vessel, carrying containers only for India, will sail a longer distance if it drops its cargo at Great Nicobar instead of Colombo and a shorter distance if it drops its cargo at Great Nicobar instead of Singapore. However, if its cargo is not wholly for India then it will only make a minor detour of 40 nautical miles. Similar calculations operate for west-bound ships. What is more incontrovertible is that, in both cases, feeder vessels will save travel time and distance.

The counterargument about strategic considerations comes with its own questions. Does a defence project have to be clubbed with a transshipment port, a tourism hub and a financial city?

How does one understand these choices?

Like airlines, shipping firms increasingly follow a hub-and-spoke model. Their largest vessels—like Ultra Large Container Vessels—drop containers heading to India's eastern seaboard at transshipment ports in Colombo, Port Klang or Singapore. These ships, which continue to grow in size as shippers chase efficiency, do not deviate from their route. 'It is not cost-effective for them to do so,' said the maritime consultant. 'They drop cargo at a transshipment port from where it is moved by a smaller ship to the destination.'

This is where the claimed opportunity for Great Nicobar lies. 'While Chennai will find it cheaper to source containers from Colombo, for ports like Vizag, Gangavaram, Paradeep, Kolkata, and even Bangladesh and Myanmar, Nicobar is closer than Singapore,' said the maritime consultant.

Indeed, a feeder vessel dropping (and collecting) containers to and from Great Nicobar and Singapore will cut sailing distance by close to 1,000 nautical miles—a saving of as much as $150 per container, said the consultant—in a line where, as websites like Freightos show, the cost of shipping a container to Vizag currently stands at $5,241 (Germany), $4,345 (New York) and $2,874 (Guangdong). With a base at Great Nicobar, the argument goes, shipping revenues to and from India will stay within the country, rather than go to Singapore and Colombo. In addition, the country can start handling some of the container traffic between Bangladesh and Myanmar.

Sailing distance, however, is not the only factor that shipping lines consider when determining where to offload containers. 'Many of these ships are going around the Cape of Good Hope,' the head of a shipping industry association told *Frontline* on condition of anonymity. 'Another day's sail doesn't matter. The number one factor is the draft; then space to keep container cargo for a week or ten days before other vessels come to collect it; then the capacity to berth vessels up to 425 metres long.'

Apart from these, he said, productivity is important. 'In industry standards, the turnaround time for a vessel with 10,000 TEUs (twenty-foot equivalent unit) is twenty-four hours at the most. Then there are port charges; this includes vessel charges and container handling charges.'

A 2022 paper published in the journal *Marine Policy* echoes this. Titled 'Do Container Terminal Operators and Liner Shipping Companies See Eye to Eye?', the paper says: 'For port operators, the most important criterion for competitiveness is port location, followed by service level, port tariffs, and port facilities. In contrast, the most important criterion for carriers is (port) operational efficiency.'

Finally, as mentioned, transshipment ports don't exist in isolation. 'Before a shipping line decides to shift its transshipment business, it will need bunkering, crane operators, banks, hotels, staff housing, schools, hospitals and power plants,' said the maritime consultant. 'If we are talking about 3.5 million containers, that is 280 ships a year. Each will need support services, immigration, crew changes, airline coverage, pilotage, customs and so on.'

Great Nicobar passes the first of these tests—its draft is 20 metres. The next three requirements are construction challenges that can be addressed. Similarly, while turnaround time for most Indian ports is high, experts say private ports are globally competitive.

Vessel charges might be a problem. The average call cost for vessels of 3,000 TEU capacity in India works out to $32,000, compared with $7,000 in Colombo, $8,000 in Singapore and $12,000 in Hong Kong. 'All Indian ports have high vessel charges,' said the head of the shipping association. The reasons, he said, besides high fixed costs, are running costs like labour, pensions and dredging. In private ports, there is the added possibility of rising monopolisation pushing charges up.

Port charges, however, are where the real problem lies. In the Indian Ocean region, container handling charges range between $25 and $45. 'Port charges are negotiated,' said the shipping association official, 'but $25–$35 is what Colombo will charge; Singapore might be $10 more.' To attract vessels, Great Nicobar will have to offer similar rates. 'It doesn't matter what the fixed cost is,' he said. 'If they want business, they will have to be competitive. Otherwise, even if they build a Taj Mahal, ships won't come.'

In its Preliminary Engineering Design Report for the International Container transshipment Terminal (ICTT) at Galathea Bay, engineering consultancy AECOM made a similar point. While Great Nicobar can levy similar vessel charges as Colombo, the report says, its terminal handling charges (THC) have to be lower. 'For GNI [Great Nicobar Island] to become a serious force, the landed cost of containers should be competitive if not lower than the region's other transshipment terminals ... It is proposed that GNI start with a tariff discount of 20% on the tariff offered by Colombo. Hence, the recommended THC tariff for GNI is $32.8/TEU-move.'

Now, the project's Environmental Impact Assessment (EIA) report pegs the cost of the transshipment terminal at Rs 35,959 crore—revised last year to Rs 41,000 crore. It will be built in two phases with the first phase costing Rs 18,000 crore, and its capacity will be 4 million containers. It is projected to be built up by 2028. By 2059, the port capacity will quadruple to 16 million containers.

Even assuming that Great Nicobar draws 4 million containers—not easy given Colombo's competitiveness plus India's push for multiple transshipment ports, each also competing with Colombo—it will make, even at $35 per container, about Rs 1,200 crore as gross revenue. At 12 per cent, interest payments alone on Rs 18,000 crore will be Rs 2,160 crore. Even if India gets cheaper loans—say, at 9 per cent—interest payments alone will stand at Rs 1,620 crore.

With such numbers, the port cannot recover its investment. This, however, is just the start. Factor in the township, and interest payments swell further. Even at 9 per cent, on a total investment of Rs 81,000 crore, annual interest payments will be Rs 7,290 crore. At 12 per cent, it will be Rs 9,720 crore.

The government's response to these mismatches has been two-fold. To make the port viable, it is putting state money into the project. A Special Purpose Vehicle (SPV) comprising Deendayal Port Authority, Paradip Port Authority and V.O. Chidambaranar Port Authority has been formed. Mumbai's Jawaharlal Nehru Port Trust was also asked to participate, with a Rs 1,400 crore investment as equity, but it baulked, citing its Vadhavan port commitment.

The SPV might borrow against its equity. Alternatively, as the head of a Port Blair–based business group said, the Centre might fund the project from the national budget. The money will go into developing basic port infrastructure like the breakwater. 'If the project is for Rs 18,000 crore, this allocation will take care of Rs 14,000 crore,' he said. 'The concessionaire will only have to pay

Rs 4,000 crore. That is like a subsidy of 70 per cent. It will make the project viable.'

This idea might have come from the AECOM report which, noting that even the port as a standalone entity (not factoring in the city) has low rates of return, suggested the government take over a part of the costs. After describing three approaches—one where the private party develops the whole project with viability gap funding from the government; another where the whole project is developed by the government; and a third where the government builds the basic infrastructure while the concessionaire runs the port and gives the state a 53 per cent revenue share—AECOM recommended the third approach. It would, it said, make the project 'financially viable for the concessionaire'.

This approach comes with its own questions. 'The best way to establish feasibility is to ask some transshipment port guy to come in and invest money,' said the businessman in Port Blair. 'They will invest if the port is viable. What we have here is the government saying it will support it.'

Given that decision, other questions follow. Given that the SPV has three firms with experience of running ports, why does India need a private concessionaire? If port trusts or the government put in Rs 14,000 crore, how do they recover that money? Conversely, if they get a 53 per cent revenue share from the concessionaire, as the AECOM report suggests, how does the port pay for itself? The AECOM study lists annual Operation and Maintenance (O&M) costs for each stage of development. These start at Rs 502 crore (2025–34) before rising to Rs 822 crore (2035–44), Rs 1,137 crore (2045–54) and Rs 1,703 crore (2055–65). In other words, if the port pulls in Rs 2,160 crore revenue (phase 1) but spends Rs 502 crore on O&M and hands another Rs 1,144.8 crore to the government, the concessionaire will be left with Rs 513.2 crore—from which it has to repay its own loans (Rs 480 crore at a commercial lending rate of 12 per cent on Rs 4,000 crore) and support the township which will have its own interest payments and O&M costs. These numbers don't add up.

Frontline shared these calculations with ANIIDCO, AECOM and the Ministry of Home Affairs (which is steering the project), for comment. As of going to press, there has been no response.

Then, there is the township. Here too, the government is pushing a part of the expenditure on to state bodies.

For instance, NTPC will build the gas-based power plant, which will cost at least Rs 3,000 crore. It isn't clear how the other amenities—schools, hospitals, hotels, housing—will be funded. Some of these, like housing, might be pure EPC (Engineering, Procurement and Construction) deals where the government pays for construction. Others, like hotels, might be handed to firms, with the government providing only basic urban infrastructure.

The government is also trying to boost other activities on the island. There is talk of developing Great Nicobar into a financial hub; a tourist destination (the airport capacity is pegged at 2 million passengers); a shipyard, a cruise terminal, but questions surround all these plans.

Plans for a financial hub—on the lines of Singapore or Macau—are fraught. Between the airport, the power plant and the port, India will spend Rs 47,000 crore. That leaves Rs 34,000 crore for the city projected to house at least 3,00,000 people. Investments in Singapore or Colombo were of a different order of magnitude altogether. The city will have to be built fast; urban amenities like hotels, hospitals, homes, shops and schools would be required from the start. So, those investments will need to be made upfront. *Frontline* asked ANIIDCO and the Ministry of Home Affairs if the government will extend viability gap funding in these cases too but received no response.

Tourism is another part of the Great Nicobar project. But, 'last year, all of Andaman and Nicobar attracted 5 lakh tourists,' said the business head in Port Blair. How many can Great Nicobar attract on its own—especially after its biggest tourist destination, Galathea Bay, is concretised into a transshipment port?

Or take the shipbuilding yard. Its competitiveness will suffer from the 2.5–3 times jump in construction costs on the archipelago. And then, there is ship repair. While it is needed for the transshipment port, it is a polluting activity that militates against the tourism plans.

If these revenue streams fail to materialise, the government might have to provide viability gap funding for the township, power plant and airport too. In that case, between rising fixed costs, interest payments and viability gap funding, what will be India's total outlay on the project?

Given that ANIIDCO is the nodal agency, *Frontline* asked a senior official at its Port Blair office if the UT administration will provide viability gap funding. The official bristled. 'Andamans cannot pay VGF,' he said. 'It is too small. GoI will have to [do so].'

Such calculations have created an impression in Port Blair that the Great Nicobar project is not about the transshipment port at all. 'It doesn't feel commercial to me,' said the businessman. 'I think the logic here is more strategic than commercial.' That hypothesis, however, comes with its own questions.

From the national security perspective, the question, as retired rear admiral Raja Menon wrote in *The Indian Express*, is whether India wants a minor reconnaissance base in Great Nicobar or a full-fledged Pearl Harbour as the outpost of a future Eastern theatre command. In defence circles, opinion is split. Some feel the Navy is better off beefing up existing infrastructure at Car Nicobar, Port

Blair and Visakhapatnam than in creating a forward post that will have its own vulnerabilities. 'I don't think the Indian Navy has much say in this,' a defence analyst told *Frontline*. 'It's a government decision. The Navy wants to focus on Karwar, which is still under development even after fifteen years, due to lack of funds. That is the only port where India can dock its aircraft carrier. It also wants to develop its Port Blair facilities.'

One counterargument here, made by another defence analyst, is that 'most islands in Andaman and Nicobar are uninhabited. There is a danger that China could occupy them.' So, India should build more infrastructure on the islands. But this is as easily done by creating locally relevant infrastructure like an industrial fishing harbour, a longstanding demand there. Instead, the country is 'over-building' on Great Nicobar, with all the economic and ecological risks it carries.

In its response, the Ministry of Defence defended the project, saying: 'While existing defence assets at Car Nicobar, INS Baaz, and Port Blair play a crucial role in India's maritime security, the new infrastructure at Great Nicobar intends to complement and enhance operational capabilities, rather than supplant ongoing projects.'

In response to a second question—on whether the base's vulnerabilities will increase due to the township around it—the Ministry wrote: 'The coexistence of defence and civilian assets, both seaports and airports, is a global best practice as it facilitates potential dual use of assets during crises. The defence assets are properly ring-fenced and the increase in the commercial and civilian activities do not make our defence assets vulnerable, as borne by the operations at Vishakapatnam and Mumbai ports.'

The Ministry also denied that India's investment in Galathea Bay comes at the cost of other naval installations. 'Needless to emphasise, the investment in ICTP does not come at the expense of existing defence infrastructure projects such as Karwar, which remain a priority within our own strategic framework.'

These answers hold a clue to how the Great Nicobar project might play out on the ground. When *Frontline* spoke to a senior infrastructure official in Mumbai, he said that at its core, Great Nicobar was a strategic project. 'Infrastructure projects need to be projected at an integrated scale to get the required institutional attention, energy and traction,' he added. 'It's the nature of infrastructure planning.'

And yet, there is also the harsh reality. 'The government has real, hard fiscal constraints irrespective of the ministry,' said the infrastructure official. 'Only the minimal components that are strategic or commercially viable will be taken up. For the rest, the plan will remain on paper till such time as the situation changes and they become viable or are prioritised for budgetary resources.'

Hardwired into this schemata is a problem. If the government is cash-strapped, as the maritime consultant said, the port-city might be built in bits and pieces, but shipping firms will relocate only if all the services are in place. And if they delay relocation, even with government subsidy, the project's calculations will go awry.

Given such risks, Great Nicobar is likely to see an EPC boom. Bidders will come to build the project—not to run it. 'Most companies that bid for the port asked for EPC contracts,' said the maritime consultant. 'They did not bid for the whole project.' Besides, he said, a clutch of consultants are adding fresh components and trying to bag contracts for presenting detailed project reports. In other words, it is possible to extract profits even from an unviable project. The country, however, will get saddled with debt and ecological devastation.

Logging illustrates that well. According to official estimates, 1 million trees are to be cut. Scientists, however, peg that number ten times higher. Even at 1 million trees, the gains will be sizeable. The forests of Great Nicobar have softwoods and hardwoods.

'Hardwood can fetch as much as Rs 2,00,000 per cubic metre,' said a Port Blair–based hotelier. 'Even the softwood—like rubber—can be treated and used for furniture.'

―――――•―――――

Walking around Galathea Bay, one sees towering trees. 'There are big, big trees there,' agreed a Nicobarese tribal leader. Even assuming that one cubic metre will be logged from each tree, the timber will fetch anywhere from Rs 15,000 crore to Rs 20,000 crore if sold raw, without processing into more expensive products like veneer. If the number of trees felled is ten-fold higher, as scientists say they would be, these numbers will rise proportionately.

In other words, following from what the infrastructure official said about viability shaping the project's rollout, whether the port or township come up or not, trees will get cut. Interestingly, logging will not be done by the forest department. ANIIDCO is overseeing it. A bunch of private firms like Ultra Tech, Hyderabad-based Falcon Resilient Infra, Mumbai-based Terracon Ecotech, Delhi-based EQMS Global, and public sector undertakings like MECON, RITES and Konkan Railway Corporation Ltd have participated in its tender. It will be educative to see what percentage of the timber's value comes to the government.

As things stand, logging will further push up port costs. 'The Galathea River flows into the bay,' said a former tehsildar at Great Nicobar. It is the island's largest river. 'Once you cut trees above its delta, its run-off will increase and it will carry a lot of silt,' he said. In other words, to protect the port's 20 metre draft, dredging will be needed.

AECOM's report, however, is silent on this risk. The project's environment impact assessment too is silent on the impact of siltation on local coral reefs and marine habitats, said biologist T.R. Shankar Raman.

The Indian government has advanced two reasons for the Great Nicobar project: commercial and geopolitical. Questions swirl around both. Will the port be a white elephant? Also, with the project, feeder ships will save money, but are their savings significant enough to justify the Rs 81,000 crore (not counting interest payments and viability gap funding) that India will spend? Opinion is also split on whether India needs a large defence base at Great Nicobar. Even if it does, should it be bundled with townships and tourism?

———•———

There are other questions.

As the shipping industry moves to ever larger vessels, the port of Sabang, on the other side of the Malacca Straits in Indonesia's western extreme, will become more competitive with its draft of 40 metres. Adani was even in talks with Indonesian authorities for this port. Then, there are other risks like cost overruns, earthquakes, storms, tsunamis and political risk. 'If the government changes, this project will get abandoned,' said a Campbell Bay–based businessman. 'The government is moving fast because they do not know how long they will be in power.'

What one sees here is the political economy of infrastructure projects in India. Locals won't gain from the project. Even the settlers, as the Campbell Bay businessman told *Frontline*, will meet the same fate as the villagers of Havelock up north in the Andamans. They will have to leave. 'This project will help locals only in the short term,' he said. 'The jobs created will not go to locals. That is what happened in Havelock. The locals left after the hotels came.' Even local companies in Port Blair won't gain; the tenders are too large for them. The businessmen *Frontline* spoke to hoped for some sub-contracting work but were unsure of larger benefits. 'All profits from Great Nicobar will be repatriated to the Centre,' said a construction firm owner. 'There will be little impact on the rest of the islands.'

What Indians are getting, instead, is a big budget EPC boom that will benefit a few conglomerates.

Interestingly, the project, described as critical to India's maritime and defence interests, is not being handled by either the Ministry of Shipping or the Ministry of Defence. Instructions to ANIIDCO, instead, are coming from Amit Shah's Ministry of Home Affairs.

(First published in *Frontline*, 3 March 2025.)

3

An Airport with Red Flags

Suman S.

The Great Nicobar Island, the southernmost in the Andaman and Nicobar Island complex in the Bay of Bengal, is at the heart of numerous proposed projects that threaten the people, ecology and biodiversity of the island. Among the list of proposed projects is the Greenfield International Airport, part of the 'Holistic Development of Great Nicobar' that is to be developed over a five-year period, at an estimated cost of Rs 10,359 crores.

But the airport's development and construction clash with the rights of residents, endanger the biodiversity of the area as well as the livelihoods and survival of indigenous tribal communities, and point to potential conflicts of interest in the clearances given to the airport by government agencies. Concerns also abound regarding the intended use of the airport, and in the legality of the land allocated for the site of the airport.

Land Concerns

In the realm of construction, the term 'greenfield' refers to a land where no previous development has taken place. As per the Environmental Impact Assessment (EIA) report of the project, the 8.45 square kilometres of the area demarcated for the airport—in the southeastern part of the island—partly consists of 'vacant land', 'submerged land' and 'land owned by the government'.

The remaining land is privately owned: 234 families (of mostly ex-servicemen who were settled here by the government) living in two revenue villages—Gandhi Nagar and Shastri Nagar in Great Nicobar tehsil—use it for agriculture, residential and commercial purposes. It is for the acquisition of this private land of 4.048 square kilometres that the Delhi-based Probe Research and Social Development Pvt. Ltd (PRSD), which was awarded the tender at Rs 21,73,475 on 11 March 2024 carried out a Social Impact Assessment (SIA).

The draft of the SIA report was submitted to the Directorate of Social Welfare, Andaman and Nicobar Administration, the local body tasked with conducting the public hearing which was held in the respective villages on 28 June 2024. The hearing had been postponed twice, after concerned citizens and journalists pointed out the violation of SIA rules, including the fact that the SIA report has to be made available in the local language at least three weeks before a public hearing. The pramukh of the Gram Panchayat, in his letter to the Director of Social Welfare dated 7 June 2024, also asked for the hearing to be held in July so that the concerned stakeholders settled elsewhere could reach the island on time for the hearing. He further made a case that the project will have a huge impact on the lives of not just the residents of the affected villages but all islanders of Great Nicobar as well as the neighbouring Little Nicobar Island.

Unclear Intentions

The 6,000 Peak Hour Passenger (PHP, which means that the terminal can process 6,000 passengers at a particular time) International Airport is one of the four components of the 'Holistic Development of Great Nicobar'. The airport clubbed with an International Container Transshipment Terminal (ICTT), a power plant and a township area were all granted an Environmental and CRZ Clearance by the MoEFCC on 11 November 2022.

During the public hearing of the EIA of the project held on 27 January 2022, the airport was described as Greenfield International Airport. However, during the appraisal of the EIA process, in the 297th meeting of the Expert Appraisal Committee (EAC-Infra-I) held in May 2022, it was stated that as per the directive of the Ministry of Home Affairs, the airport will be developed as a joint military–civil dual-use airport under the operational control of the Indian Navy.

Consequently, the deliberations of the EAC regarding the impact of the airport were not made public in the minutes of the committee's meetings or the subsequent correspondence that led to the environmental clearance of the project. Moreover, by citing the airport's status, important details such as the method of enumeration of trees to be cut for the project were not mentioned in Form-2 (a crucial document for getting environmental clearance) and denied when an activist sought the information through an Right to Information (RTI) application later. Now, the draft SIA report has no mention of the status of the airport and again describes it as an international airport mainly targeted at boosting tourism and improving connectivity to the island.

Table 2: Land for the Airport

Total area of the airport	8.45 sq. km
Land to be acquired by filling the sea	0.71 sq. km
Land falling under ICRZ-IA	0.57 sq. km
Land falling under ICRZ-IB	0.82 sq. km
Land falling under ICRZ-III (No Development Zone)	0.38 sq. km
Land falling under ICRZ-IV	0.70 sq. km
Forest and Deemed Forest land*	1.41 sq. km

Source: Revised effective area under ICRZ submitted by the project proponent and the recommendation letter by ANCZMA provided to MoEFCC on 8 July 2022.
* Final EIA Report, Chapter 2(B), Vimta Labs Pvt. Ltd, March 2022.

Airplanes in, Corals out

While much has been written about the social and environmental impact of the Rs 35,959 crore ICTT port, the site of the airport too is riddled with grave environmental violations. Parts of the airport site have swathes of primary rainforest that will be clear-felled. But no information on the number of trees to be axed for the airport is available in the public domain. Even the draft SIA report, which enlists the species and number of trees that will be 'affected' due to the land acquisition, only mentions trees such as coconut, betel nut, mango, guava and other fruit-bearing trees planted by residents on their properties. However, there is a curious mention of 'wooden trees' in the list which amounts to 2,731 individuals. There is no mention in any project documents if these trees are the rainforest trees that are to be logged to make way for the airport.

The Great Nicobar Island, where the projects are proposed, serves as a stopover for many migratory birds, especially wetland birds. In the EIA report, as a measure to prevent bird hazard, the Zoological Survey of India (ZSI) has suggested removing all fruit-bearing trees within 1 kilometre of the airport boundary, and using crackers and ultrasonic waves to scare the birds. However, in listing out the impact of the airport on migratory birds, ZSI denies that Great Nicobar falls under any migratory route, contradicting their own 2018 article where they report that the archipelago comes under the East Asian Australasian Bird Flyway and supports good numbers of transcontinental migratory birds during September to March.

While the Galathea Bay beach (site of the port) due to its gradual slope and finer sands is visited by hundreds of giant leatherback turtles to lay eggs every year, the beaches of both Gandhi Nagar and Shastri Nagar, where the airport is proposed, are predominantly visited by the green sea, olive ridley and hawksbill turtles every year. The impact of land reclamation on these beaches and the turtles has not been assessed by the Wildlife Institute of India (WII), which was tasked with analysing the eco-sensitivity of the beaches in Great Nicobar in the context of the proposed project. As per an article in *The Times of India* published on 30 July 2024, scientists at WII have admitted that the impact of the airport on the turtle nesting beaches is yet to be assessed, but the project was still granted clearance.

The beach in Gandhi Nagar supports seventy-six species of Scleractinian or 'stony' corals and the beach in Shastri Nagar harbors 111 species of these corals: the beach has an area of 1.04 square kilometres under reef cover. The ZSI study that is a part of the EIA report states that coral colonies impacted by dredging and land reclamation for the port and the airport will be translocated to other sites on the island with a similar environment. However, in a subsequent report titled 'Conservation and Management Plan for Coral Reefs of Great Nicobar Island' submitted to the EAC in

July 2022, the beach in Gandhi Nagar, which will also be dredged to accommodate the runway, thereby damaging the corals, is listed as the location where the corals removed from Galathea Bay will be transplanted.

Similarly, the WII, in their 'Conservation and Management Plan of Saltwater Crocodile in Great Nicobar Island' submitted in July 2022, states that the runway requires reclamation of the wetland where there are crocodiles. The plan is to translocate these crocodiles and radio-tag them to monitor their movements—'if' they are released in the wild. However, the impact of the crocodile relocation on the ecology of the water bodies where these crocodiles will be released is not mentioned anywhere in the report. The altered river ecology will in turn have an impact on the diet of the Shompen, who derive a substantial amount of their food from rivers and creeks.

As for the ground-nesting Nicobar megapode, the mounds of about nine to sixteen birds that live in the proximity of the airport will be permanently destroyed. The Salim Ali Centre for Ornithology and Natural History (SACON), a WII subsidiary, in its 'Comprehensive Plan for Nicobar Megapode Conservation in the Nicobar Archipelago' submitted to the EAC in May 2022, suggests the relocation and captive management for this shy, elusive bird whose numbers took a plunge post-tsunami and are still dwindling. The management plan budgets building a temporary holding enclosure that exactly resembles the megapodes' natural habitat, adding that the injured birds or those that are unable to relocate will be kept in captivity for 'restocking'.

Conflicts of Interest

The WII, ZSI and SACON—the very organisations whose reports formed the basis of the Environmental and CRZ Clearance granted to the project—have been entrusted with the preparation and implementation of wildlife conservation plans for a collective budget of Rs 2,017.63 crores as per the minutes of the joint meeting of monitoring committees responsible for the implementation of Environment Management Plan for Great Nicobar held on 31 March 2023.

Interestingly, as per the minutes, the conservation plans are being sent to the Ministry of Home Affairs before going to the MoEFCC for approvals. There is a complete lack of transparency and ignorance towards fulfilling the conditions laid out in the environmental clearance. For instance, the aforementioned minutes of the joint meeting had to be procured through an RTI even when the environmental clearance issued to the project had clearly stated that the minutes of such meetings must be put up on the website of the Department of Environment and Forest of Andaman and Nicobar.

Despite over a hundred ex-bureaucrats appealing for a fair and thorough SIA, and the Indian National Congress demanding the suspension of the environmental and forest clearances granted to the project, the public hearing for the SIA of the airport was held on 28 June 2024 at the community halls of the respective affected villages. According to a few attendees who were present in the hearing, most ex-servicemen settlers seemed to have no objections with their land being acquired for the airport. However, they raised concerns over the lack of information about the location of the rehabilitation, and the circle rate (the minimum property registration value evaluated by the government) for the land in Shastri Nagar (Rs 113 per square metre) being lower than that in Gandhi Nagar (Rs 131 per square metre).

While some participants opined that they should be settled in Campbell Bay (the administrative hub of the island), others wished to be allocated land next to the airport, and given preference for running any commercial establishments that may crop up in the premises once the construction is over. Some of the other concerns raised during the hearing were demands for a fair compensation for the felling of coconut and areca nut trees as well as a provision for adequate land to keep farm animals. In response to these comments, the conducting body—which comprised of representatives from the Directorate of Social Welfare, PRSD (the agency that conducted the SIA), ANIIDCO (the project proponent) and the members of the village Gram Panchayat—said that an Expert Committee will be formed to conduct the land acquisition, resettlement and rehabilitation of the two affected villages and all the issues raised during the meeting will be addressed by the committee.

As per some of the written objections that were submitted by civilian groups, the independence of the agency conducting the SIA, PRSD, is questionable as the members of the project proponent, ANIIDCO, were involved in its selection. As per the Social Impact Assessment and Consent Rules, 2013, an independent body unconnected to government bodies should have been at the helm, and ANIIDCO should not have been involved. Despite heavy criticism from various groups, the final SIA report was submitted in July 2024.

In September 2024, an independent multidisciplinary expert group submitted the evaluation report of the SIA conducted for the airport. The seven-member group comprised the Assistant Commissioner, two representatives of the Gram Panchayats, Executive Engineer from the Public Works Department, the Associate Town and Country Planner as well as two social scientists from Indian Institute of Technology Kharagpur and Tata Institute of Social Sciences, Mumbai. In its observations, the expert group has stated: 'The project will result in the displacement of several local communities, including farmers and landowners who have resided in the affected areas for generations. This displacement will not only impact their homes but also disrupt long-established social and cultural ties.' It concluded that the benefits of the project outweigh the associated social costs.

However, the local communities mentioned here are the settlers from the mainland. Unfortunately, the expert members failed to acknowledge the existence of the Shompen and Nicobarese people—two indigenous communities who have resided on the island for over thousands of years—and their dependence on the forest land that is to be acquired for the project. This resulted in their exclusion from the SIA study.

All these issues put together raise numerous red flags regarding the proposed greenfield airport on Great Nicobar Island, the legality of the land allocated for it, the airport's intended use, and the impact it could have on the people and biodiversity of the island.

(First published in The Wire, *2 August 2024. This updated version reflects the latest situation.)*

4

What Do We Know About ANIIDCO?

Pankaj Sekhsaria and Rishika Pardikar

Why has the qualifications of the Andaman and Nicobar Islands Integrated Development Corporation (ANIIDCO) come into question after it got permission for a Rs 72,000 crore mega infrastructure project in Great Nicobar? Does the company have a proper internal environmental governance system?

The Story So Far

ANIIDCO is the project proponent for the NITI Aayog–promoted Rs 72,000 crore mega infrastructure project in Great Nicobar, the southernmost island in the Andaman and Nicobar archipelago. The project entails the construction of a transshipment port, a greenfield airport, a tourism and township project, and a solar- and gas-based power plant in Great Nicobar. ANIIDCO, which has been granted permission for the megaproject, is a little-known quasi-government agency based in Port Blair.

What We Do Know About ANIIDCO?

ANIIDCO was incorporated on 28 June 1988 under the Companies Act. Its objective is 'to develop and commercially exploit natural resources for the balanced and environment friendly development of the territory.' Its main activities, according to its website, include trading of petroleum products, Indian made foreign liquor and milk, managing tourism resorts and infrastructure development for tourism and fisheries.

The company's average annual turnover and profit over the last three financial years has been Rs 370 crore and Rs 35 crore, respectively. The corporation's mandate, history, its structure and capabilities raise serious concerns about the process and possible outcomes of making them responsible for such a high profile, high investment and high risk project as the one in Great Nicobar. The 910 square kilometres island is not just a biodiversity hotspot but also home to indigenous communities with special rights and is also located in one of the most tectonically active zones.

When the Andaman and Nicobar administration appointed ANIIDCO as project proponent in July 2020, ANIIDCO neither had an environment policy nor an environment cell. It did not even have the human resources needed to oversee, let alone implement and monitor the project it was tasked to implement. It was only in late 2022—more than two years after it was made the project proponent—that it started a process for recruiting people with relevant expertise such as urban planners, environmental planners, architects, infrastructure specialists, and legal and financial experts.

In May 2021, the Expert Appraisal Committee (EAC) under the Union Ministry of Environment, Forest and Climate Change had asked ANIIDCO a number of important questions about its internal environmental governance system. The EAC asked if ANIIDCO had a corporate environment policy approved by its board of directors, an administrative system to ensure compliance with environmental clearance conditions, and if there was a prescribed standard operating procedure to deal with environmental and forest violations. In August of the same year, ANIIDCO admitted that it did not have an environment policy. The EAC, nevertheless, went ahead and granted environmental clearance to ANIIDCO more than a year later, in November 2022.

Other Conflicts of Interests

In 2022, the Mumbai-based Conservation Action Trust had filed a petition before the National Green Tribunal (NGT) challenging the Stage 1 forest clearance granted to the project by the Union Ministry of Environment, Forest and Climate Change. It had pointed out that at the time forest clearance was granted to ANIIDCO, the corporation's Managing Director was the same person as the Commissioner cum Secretary (Environment and Forests) of the island.

It is clear, the petition noted, that this is 'a case of the project proponent certifying itself.' Further, it added that the responsibility to assess compliance with the Stage 1 forest clearance conditions vests with the same authority that has a responsibility to ensure compliance with the conditions. This same pattern was repeated when the Chief Secretary of the islands, who is also the Chairman of the board of directors of ANIIDCO, was made a key member of the high-powered committee set up by the NGT to look into complaints against the project.

ANIIDCO was being allowed to evaluate its own actions again. Numerous persons employed at ANIIDCO in various capacities are currently civil servants with the Andaman and Nicobar administration in charge of environmental and tribal welfare issues. We sent questionnaires to both ANIIDCO, and theChairman and Secretary of the EAC. None responded.

From Past Administrators

Lt Gen. A.K. Singh, Lt Governor of the islands from 2013 to 2016, said that ANIIDCO would be better suited than any other department or organisation in the Andaman and Nicobar administration to handle this megaproject, though a project of this dimension would require expert agencies from outside the islands to execute it.

Sanat Kaul, Chief Secretary of the islands in the early 1990s, had critiqued ANIIDCO's tourism operations in his book *Andaman and Nicobar Islands: India's Untapped Strategic Assets*, published in 2015. On the current project, he said, 'I don't think ANIIDCO can at all manage a Rs 72,000 crore project unless it is upgraded vastly with much better quality staff. If the idea of the government is to use ANIIDCO because it is an existing company fully owned by the government, it will need a full revamp from what it was when I was there.'

(First published in *The Hindu*, 5 September 2024.)

INDIGENOUS LANDSCAPES

5

Tribal Lands Don't Show Up on Maps

Rishika Pardikar

We are in Barnabas Manju's office, a one-bedroom house in a government quarter in Campbell Bay. He is the Chairman of the Tribal Council of Great Nicobar and Little Nicobar. A long-pending demand of the Tribal Council is for a formal office with work equipment. 'There is nothing here. No computers to work. We just have a chair,' Barnabas said.

From a demand for a formal office to answers on a megaproject that threatens to destroy their way of life, Barnabas Manju is stonewalled and his visitors surveilled. It is daytime but we are sitting in the dark with the curtains closed and the lights turned off because the local police and Intelligence Bureau (IB) are tracking us.

The bureaucratic juggernaut is slowly but surely rolling ahead with plans for a Rs 81,000 crore project on the island of Great Nicobar, which is home to two tribal communities—the almost completely isolated Shompen and the Nicobarese—and numerous endemic plant and animal species. A majority of the island today is covered by rainforests, which are part of the Sundaland biodiversity hotspot extending to Southeast Asia. It includes places like Borneo, Java and Sumatra.

When a Social Impact Assessment (SIA) was commissioned for the project that held deep ramifications for the tribes' habitats, neither Barnabas nor others from the Nicobarese community were invited to the discussions.

Spearheaded by the Union Ministry of Home Affairs, the project comprises a transshipment terminal, an international airport, gas and solar power plants, a township and high-end tourism facilities. While it is already in the final stage of gaining statutory approvals, more plans are being revealed, such as an international cruise terminal. Companies like Adani Ports, JSW Infrastructure, Megha Engineering & Infrastructures Ltd and Navayuga Engineering Co. Ltd have reportedly expressed interest in operating and running the transshipment terminal.

The island, which has not entirely recovered from the devastating tsunami of 2004, is now at the mercy of a determined Union government that refuses to answer questions about the project and routinely denies information sought under the Right to Information Act, citing Section 8(1)(a), which states 'information, disclosure of which would prejudicially affect the sovereignty and integrity of India, the security, strategic, scientific or economic interests of the State, relation with foreign State or lead to incitement of an offence' can be denied. The local administration is also equally tight-lipped about the project.

The Assistant Commissioner, who is the executive head for the island of Great Nicobar, denied multiple requests for an interview. Local forest officials in the Nicobar division of the Andaman and Nicobar Forest Department too did not wish to speak about the project, while one officer in particular, the Assistant Conservator of Forests, said the project is covered by the Official Secrets Act and he will not be engaging in any discussions about it.

Even as approvals are being given, there is no estimate of which tribal villages, and hunting and foraging grounds will be taken over or of the social impact of such a takeover on the two communities.

The only way to realise which tribal areas are set to be lost to the project is if one looks at a twenty-year-old map (see Map 3) prepared by researcher Manish Chandi, for there has never been any systematic governmental effort to map tribal lands in Great Nicobar either. In fact, the map in a feasibility report prepared for the project in March 2021 completely ignored tribal settlements and foraging areas and chose to show only national forests, forest reserves and revenue lands.

There is a clear overlap of the project area and tribal lands when compared with the map prepared by Chandi.

As criticism from all quarters has mounted about the megaproject for the havoc it will wreak, the administration has maintained an eagle eye over its people and outsiders, especially journalists. Our movements were tracked as soon as we arrived in Campbell Bay. Our interview with the Nicobarese community in the tribal colony in Rajiv Nagar was once stopped by a jeep full of police and IB personnel. The local Forest Department also denied us permission to visit Galathea Bay, the proposed site of the transshipment terminal, though it was open to Indian government officials and even tourists.

Unmapped Tribal Lands to Be Taken Over for the Project

The autochthonous tribes of Shompen and Nicobarese have lived on the island of Great Nicobar for thousands of years. The Shompen are a semi-nomadic, hunter-gatherer community and they live deep in the forests in Great Nicobar. They are, by and large, isolated from the rest of the population on the island. They

Map 3: A hand-drawn map titled 'Great Nicobar Island and surrounding places in Payuh geography', compiled by Manish Chandi (ANET, 2000–04). The map marks various tribal place names and geographical features across the island, including Puloluon, Komgvengeh, ReKinchen, ReAnanso, Rekoret, ReReuieh and many others, highlighting traditional Nicobarese toponyms.

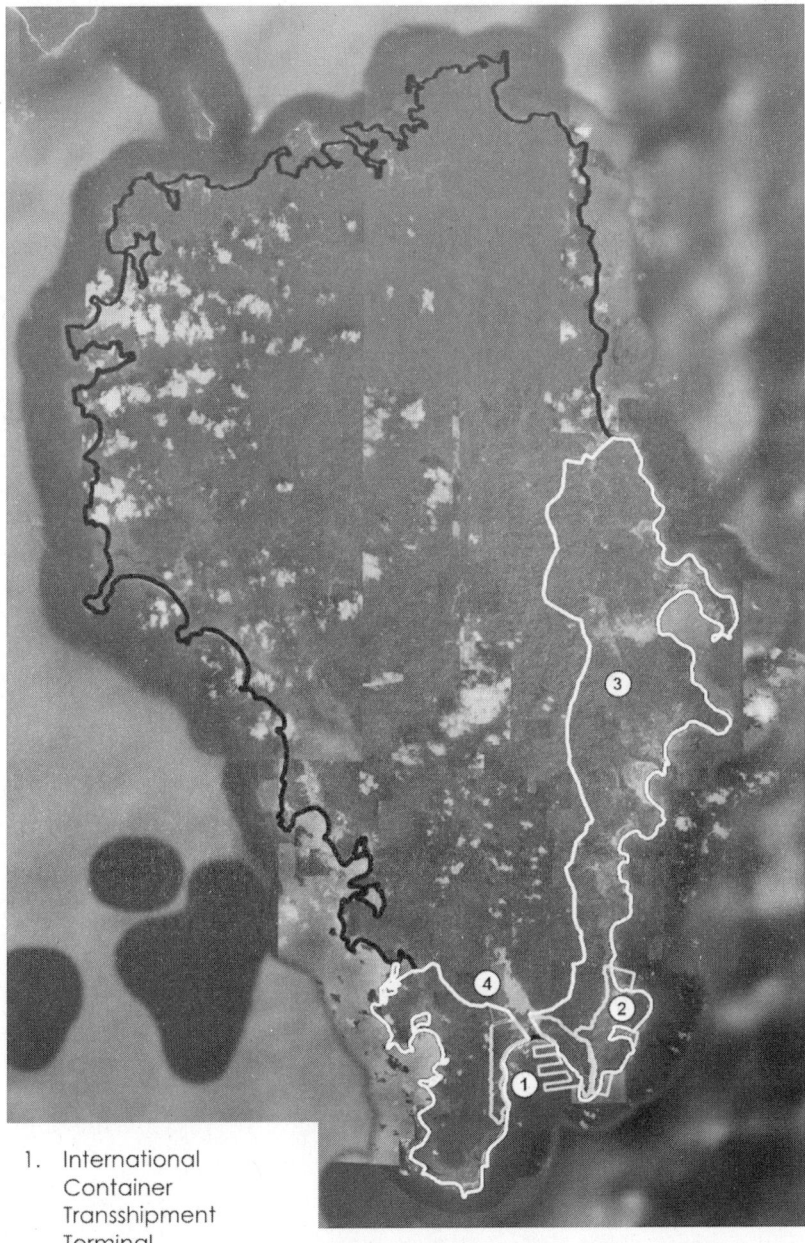

1. International Container Transshipment Terminal
2. International Airport
3. Township and Area Development
4. Power Plant

Map 4: Great Nicobar Island with different components of the project mapped out.

Source: Pre-feasibility report prepared by AECOM, titled 'Holistic Development of Great Nicobar Island at Andaman & Nicobar Islands'

are a particularly vulnerable tribal group with a population of just around 250 people.

The Nicobarese are also a tribal community but they are largely a settled population. They grow plantations, fish and hunt, and in recent years, they have also taken up daily wage work to make a living. They are spread across the Nicobar Islands like Car Nicobar, Little Nicobar and Great Nicobar. The population of the Nicobarese in Great Nicobar is about 1,200.

In the Nicobarese language, the Great Nicobar Island is called 'Patai Takaru', meaning 'the big island', because, with an area of 920 square kilometres, the island is the biggest one in the Nicobar group of islands. We do not know how the Shompen conceptualise their land and forests because their language has not been deciphered yet.

The project will displace Nicobarese and Shompen communities whose way of life is closely connected to their lands. It will take over forests comprising settled villages and areas used for foraging, hunting and plantations. Like Chingenh, Kirasis and Kurchinom in Galathea Bay; In Haengloi and Pulo Baha in Pemmaya Bay; and Kokeon, Bui Jayae and Pulo Pakka in Nanjappa Bay.

'All these villages will go when the project comes. These are all tribal villages,' Barnabas said, pointing to the map prepared by Chandi, taped onto the wall in his office. Chandi prepared the map between 2000 and 2004 when he was working with the Andaman Nicobar Environment Team (ANET). Later, he went on to pursue a PhD in the field of human ecology. To date, this remains the only comprehensive map of the island that lists tribal lands.

The map shows settlements like Chingenh, In Haengloi and Kokeon along the south and southwest coasts of the island. These are ancestral villages of the Nicobarese who were settled by the government in a tribal colony in Rajiv Nagar after the 2004 tsunami. Some of these areas also belong to the Shompen. The two communities share a bartering relationship over forest and agricultural products.

In fact, Chingenh, which Barnabas pointed to on the map, is located right in the area where the transshipment terminal is proposed to be built in Galathea Bay. This location is a biodiversity hotspot and serves as one of the largest nesting sites in the world for giant leatherback turtles.

The Nicobar division of the Andaman and Nicobar Forest Department did not permit us to visit Galathea Bay even while a steady stream of tourists and government officials from the island, Port Blair and New Delhi were allowed and even escorted by the department during the same time. Many of the officials were visiting Galathea Bay for project-related work.

A 'Babu's' Idea of Demarcation

It is no secret that, for decades now, the local administration in Great Nicobar has been relying on the map prepared by Chandi to identify tribal areas. The map was used as and when it was convenient to contact the tribes but ignored when the proposed project directly threatened the tribes' way of life.

The maps that have been used to plan the megaproject do not list lands used by the two tribal communities. This, even while it seeks to take over such lands. This disingenuity reveals that no attempt was made to sincerely assess the impact of the land acquisition on the affected communities or be deterred by the protections that covered the land. The rescue and relief efforts after the tsunami of 2004 relied heavily on Chandi's map to locate tribal areas. In fact, the office of the then Assistant Commissioner in Campbell Bay specifically requested Chandi's help in locating tribal communities and their villages. Chandi also provided details of tribal community demographics and land ownership patterns.

After 2004, he added more Nicobarese settlements and Shompen community areas to this map. However, given that these are efforts undertaken by one individual, the map is not exhaustive. It is safe to assume that there are many more unmapped tribal settlements and foraging grounds, more so those belonging to the Shompen community.

This reporter visited and spoke to various officials from the Andaman and Nicobar administration, such as the office of the Assistant Commissioner (Campbell Bay), the Nicobar division of the Forest Department and the Directorate of Tribal Welfare. None of them possessed maps where tribal settlements and foraging grounds were marked. Every office only displayed maps with broad boundaries like revenue areas, tribal reserves and national parks.

'The government has no proper map of tribal areas. There has been no systematic mapping effort,' said Vishvajit Pandya, an anthropologist and Director of Andaman Nicobar Tribal Research Institute under the Ministry of Tribal Affairs. 'They use vague language like "upper road Shompen" and "lower road Shompen". And these roads have been washed away in the [2004] tsunami! It's a babu's idea of demarcation.' Babu, in colloquial Hindi, means a bureaucrat.

Even the Anthropological Survey of India (AnSI), including its regional centre in Andaman and Nicobar, does not have a map that chalks out lands belonging to the Shompen and the Nicobarese in Great Nicobar. This was confirmed by Anstice Justin, a Nicobarese anthropologist and former deputy director of AnSI. Anstice also belongs to the Nicobarese community from Car Nicobar.

Consider the report prepared by AECOM, the consultancy engaged by NITI Aayog to assess the feasibility of the megaproject. The land use map contained in this report shows the location of national parks, forest reserves and revenue lands but not tribal settlements and foraging grounds, something that is clearly shown in the map prepared by Chandi (see Map 3).

The documents submitted as part of environment clearance also listed the project only in the revenue areas of Campbell Bay, Govind Nagar, Joginder Nagar, Vijay Nagar, Laxminagar, Gandhi Nagar and Shastri Nagar, completely ignoring the fact that tribal areas will also be taken over.

No Social Impact Assessment for the Tribes

Overall, the megaproject requires 166 square kilometres of land on the island, including 130 square kilometres of forest land and 84 square kilometres designated as a tribal reserve. There is an overlap between lands designated as forest land and tribal reserves. These lands comprise settlements, ancestral lands and foraging grounds of the Nicobarese and the Shompen, as well as revenue areas where settlers from mainland states like Punjab, West Bengal, Andhra Pradesh and Tamil Nadu live.

In 1969, the then Union government settled families of ex-military servicemen from Punjab on the island, mainly for security purposes. In the following years, families of ex-servicemen from other parts of India, too, were settled on the island. Later, other people like fishermen and labourers from various parts of the country also arrived. Today, the settler population on the island is around 6,500.

Given such a scale of impact, the Directorate of Social Welfare under the Andaman and Nicobar administration sought a Social Impact Assessment (SIA) report from Probe Research and Social Development Pvt. Ltd. Not much is known about the company except that it classifies itself as engaged in 'research and experimental development on natural sciences and engineering'. It has also undertaken SIA for construction-related land acquisition in other islands like Lakshadweep.

A social impact assessment is a legal requirement under the Social Impact Assessment and Consent Rules of the Right to Fair Compensation and Transparency in Land Acquisition, Rehabilitation and Resettlement Act, 2013. But the mandate of the SIA report was limited to assessing the impact of the proposed airport, not the transshipment terminal or any of the other components of the project like the township and tourism facilities.

The final SIA report submitted by Probe Research and Social Development is also silent on the impact of the megaproject on the Nicobarese and the Shompen.

The only mention of the impact on tribal communities in the SIA report is vague. It states, 'As far as possible, the affected families shall be relocated in a similar ecological zone, so as to preserve the economic opportunities, language, and culture and community life of the tribal communities.'

Barnabas recalled, 'Nicobarese villages will be affected by the project. But they did not invite us [to SIA meetings] for discussions.'

―――・―――

A few days later, we met two women from the Nicobarese community in Barnabas's office to resume the conversation that was stopped by the police and IB at the tribal colony in Rajiv Nagar earlier. They spoke to us on the condition of anonymity. Recollecting the abrupt end of the previous meeting, one of them said, 'You had come to take our views and we wanted to share. So, why did they stop it?'

'Someone has come from outside. They want to talk to us. They will understand our problems and sadness. They will ask and we will tell them,' the other woman said. Both of them expressed fears of being removed from their land for the development of the mammoth project. 'Our views are suppressed now. When the project comes, they can remove us from here [Rajiv Nagar] also. Where will we go then?' they ask. For the Nicobarese community in Rajiv Nagar, this will mark a second displacement, the first one being in 2004 because of the tsunami.

Displacement is not new for the Shompen either. In a chapter titled 'Ignored Shompens in Hiding' in the book *Andaman and Nicobar Tribes Restudied*, Rann Singh Mann, who previously served as a director of AnSI, documents this phenomenon in detail. He writes about how the Shompen had to give up some of their land when ex-servicemen settlers were brought to the island, and with it came loss of forest resources, death due to diseases and erosion of their culture. Being a relatively isolated tribe, the Shompen are not exposed to, and therefore have not built an immunity to, diseases from mainland India. The megaproject also entails disease risks for the Shompen, given it will bring large populations from the mainland.

A few days after this, we arranged another meeting at the tribal colony in Rajiv Nagar to speak to one of the captains of a Nicobarese village that will be taken over for the project. In the Nicobarese system, captains are village heads. Speaking on the condition of anonymity, he emphasised the importance of living in their own lands. 'Our land is necessary to secure our future,' he said, referring to ancestral lands that the community would like to return to. The Nicobarese have made it clear that they would not like any development activities on their traditional lands.

Ever since the tsunami in 2004, the Nicobarese living in Rajiv Nagar have asked to be relocated to their original villages and for facilities like roads, housing and electricity to be provided there. These villages are along the south and southwest coast—some of the same areas chalked out now for the mega port like Chingen and Kokeon. The Andaman and Nicobar administration has never accepted their demands for relocation. Now, the project entails the permanent displacement of the Nicobarese from their original villages.

The captain added that he would have had no problem with the project if it were not taking over their lands. Although he does raise one concern with the project: 'The project will bring a lot of people to this island, and for them, the government can change all the rules. Tomorrow, they can tell us to vacate. Where will we go?'

Members of the community also speak about how living in Rajiv Nagar has slowly eroded their cultural practices. Earlier, festivals were celebrated for weeks and even death ceremonies were an elaborate affair. Ancestors were remembered and celebrated for months. But today, the government has not given them land to undertake plantations that could provide food for large group activities. They often have difficulty accessing forest resources for daily needs like food and building their homes. Communal practices like living in large families have also been discontinued because the tsunami shelters in Rajiv Nagar are small. As a result, they now do not celebrate festivals that last more than a day or two.

According to Anstice Justin, there was no need for the Nicobarese to work outside their villages earlier. He said, 'They had their own plantations and it was a plantation-based economy. Today, some of them work in construction as daily wage labourers. And now, the international port and tourism [planned as part of the megaproject] is not going to be useful for the Nicobarese community.'

He further added, 'It is good to develop the island and to ensure [national] security but the government has to think about the Nicobarese.' He also echoed another fear expressed by the community members and the captain: 'In the long run, I have a feeling that there will be no space for tribal people in the Andaman and Nicobar Islands, even in Great Nicobar.'

As of today, the fate of tribal communities in the Andaman group of islands is dire too. The Andaman and Nicobar administration settled the Great Andamanese on Strait Island. The tribe was earlier spread across the Andaman islands but the government has now confined them to Strait Island. The Jarawa, an Andamanese tribe, have lost a lot of their land to developmental activities that have not only not benefitted them but have also led to poaching, illegal logging and exploitation of Jarawa women. And Onge, another Andamanese tribe, is also being pushed to exclusion and marginalisation on the island of Little Andaman.

As for the Shompen, there is no way to communicate with the community because we do not understand their language. However, in one rare instance, some members of the community expressed opposition to intrusions into their forests.

In 2020, the Andaman and Nicobar administration formed an empowered committee composed of persons who have worked for decades in Great Nicobar to understand on-ground sentiments about the development of a transshipment terminal. The committee included Vishvajit Pandya, the anthropologist who earlier spoke about how no mapping exercise has been undertaken by any government agency, and Manish Chandi, the only person who has mapped tribal lands in Great Nicobar.

The video report that the committee submitted to the Andaman and Nicobar administration featured comments made by a member of the Shompen community, translated into Hindi by a Nicobarese who understands their language to a limited extent. The report has not been released publicly by the administration but some video clippings from it were included in a webinar held in 2021.

'Do not come near our hills,' one of the Shompen men says. 'If you want to cut forests, cut them along the coast. But do not climb our forests.'

This is the only glimpse that the outside world has had into what the Shompen think. However, the views expressed in the video are limited to one particular group of Shompen. The Shompen live in many small groups comprising twenty to thirty people, referred to as 'bands'. The outside world has almost no contact with the Shompen, who live deep in the forests in Great Nicobar.

Nevertheless, Probe Research and Social Development—the private company that conducted the SIA—did not take into account any such concerns expressed by the two tribal communities.

In July 2024, Probe Research and Social Development submitted the final SIA report to the Directorate of Social Welfare. The report detailed the land holdings of the settler community, the associated social and economic impacts of the project, and compensation and rehabilitation issues. The report did not present a map showing tribal settlements and steered clear of assessing impacts from taking over lands of the Nicobarese and the Shompen.

The final SIA report included detailed maps and land-use patterns in project-affected revenue areas like Gandhi Nagar and Shastri Nagar. A public hearing was also held in June 2024 to assess the sentiments of the settler community about the project and its potential impact. No such public hearings were conducted for the tribal communities.

Hasty Approvals

During the early stages of the project in 2021-22, when no impact assessments—environmental or social—had even begun, both Forest Department and Tribal Welfare Department wrote to the Andaman and Nicobar administration, assenting to the project. In fact, the Director of Tribal Welfare stated that his office is even willing to provide exemptions from the protection of Aboriginal tribes policies and regulations to ensure the execution of the project.

The then Divisional Forest Officer for the Nicobar division of the Andaman and Nicobar Forest Department said his office had no objection to the cutting of 130 square kilometres of forests for the megaproject.

For the forest clearance, a no-objection certificate (NOC) was obtained from the Tribal Council in 2022. But the council withdrew it later, stating it was obtained by providing false information that their lands would not be taken away. Barnabas Manju said the meetings were held amid Independence Day preparations and celebrations between 13 August and 16 August 2022, and he was rushed to sign the NOC. He also said that they were assured that the Nicobarese community would get all the help they needed to get settled in their pre-tsunami ancestral settlements, but it was never mentioned in the minutes of the proceedings. Today, the project is set to take over many such ancestral lands of the Nicobarese and also the forests of the Shompen.

(First published as 'Tribal Lands Don't Show Up on Maps as Union Government Pushes Mega Project', in *The News Minute*, 4 April 2025.)

6

Empower Earth's Guardians

Ajay Saini and Manish Chandi

In the southern expanse of the Andaman and Nicobar archipelago, off the shores of Little Nicobar, lie seven tiny islands. Classified as 'uninhabited' in the government's records, these islets are nonetheless integral to the indigenous communities of the region. Two, officially called Meroë and Menchal, are known as Piruii and Pingaeyak, respectively, to the Payuh, the indigenous southern Nicobarese people, who hold traditional rights over these and other islets.

For millennia, these historically isolated indigenes have relied on these islands as resource reservoirs for sustenance and protected them. Menchal is revered, used and protected under the spiritual realm called Pingaeyak (a spirit that is believed to reside on the island), prohibiting the overexploitation of resources or any undue harm to its ecosystem. Similarly, Meroë is believed to be the abode of a legendary islander community. Here, too, spiritual belief systems influence how the islanders use and protect natural resources.

Meroë and Menchal are managed by community elders as guardians and specific individual caretakers. They ensure the protection of the island's resources and sustainability. In today's world, this phenomenon goes by the name of 'conservation' and 'sustainable use', among other terms and phrases.

Conservation Colonialism

In May 2022, in complete disregard of the indigenous land ownership and management systems, the Andaman and Nicobar administration issued three public notices, announcing its intention to create three wildlife sanctuaries: a coral sanctuary at Meroë Island, a megapode sanctuary at Menchal Island and a leatherback turtle sanctuary on Little Nicobar Island.

In mid-July, the Andaman and Nicobar administration issued an order asserting that it did not receive any claims or objections from any individual regarding the land and marine areas within the three proposed sanctuaries; that no individual enjoys any rights within the boundaries of the proposed sanctuaries. And, that there will be 'restriction on the people of neighbouring area to enter into these islands ... in the national interest.'

Approximately 1,200 southern Nicobarese inhabit Patai Takaru (Great Nicobar Island) and Patai t-bhi (Little Nicobar Island), holding traditional rights over both inhabited and ostensibly 'uninhabited' islands. Yet, the Andaman and Nicobar administration neither consulted nor informed the southern Nicobarese of its plans.

Despite verbal supplications and a letter in August 2022 from the Little & Great Nicobar Tribal Council that expressed the community's concerns to the Andaman and Nicobar administration and the Ministry of Environment, Forest and Climate Change, the Andaman and Nicobar administration proceeded to issue official notifications in October 2022, designating the whole of Meroë (2.73 square kilometres, including the surrounding marine area) and Menchal (1.29 square kilometres), along with a 13.75 square kilometres area (including 6.67 square kilometres of water area within the baseline system) on Little Nicobar (140 square kilometres), as wildlife sanctuaries.

Masking an Ecological Disaster

The selection of Meroë and Menchal Islands as conservation reserves for coral reefs and megapode birds is arbitrary. Menchal does not have more than a pair or two of the endemic megapode. Similarly, questions arise regarding the actual diversity and abundance of corals on Meroë Island.

Notably, the announcement of wildlife sanctuaries coincided with growing scrutiny and criticism from experts over the denotification of the Galathea Bay Wildlife Sanctuary for a Rs 72,000 crore megaproject on Great Nicobar, a UNESCO biosphere reserve.

Establishing exclusionary conservation areas in a region which is already a paradise for biodiversity stems from the fact that the champions of the megaproject are aware of the extensive environmental and social damage that the project will entail. It will devastate about 8 lakh to 10 lakh evergreen forest trees, smother and gouge out scores of coral reefs found along Galathea Bay, destroy the nesting site for the globally endangered leatherback sea turtle species, devastate hundreds of nesting mounds of Nicobar megapodes and kill as many crocodiles.

Furthermore, it will prevent the indigenous Great Nicobar islanders from returning to their pre-tsunami homeland where they husbanded pigs and chicken, cultivated coconut and betel nut trees, and lived simple and gregarious lives. Most importantly, it will uproot three or more settlements of the Shompen (a particularly vulnerable tribal group) and permanently destroy their foraging and hunting grounds. The unilateral decision to establish wildlife sanctuaries disregards the islands' profound significance to the indigenous population. Their ancestral lands are unjustly perceived as 'no-man's-land' to appease conservationists, investors, public opinion and more.

Support Earth's Guardians

Globally, governments blatantly violate indigenous people's rights by evicting them from their ancestral lands, often under the guise of development, national interest and conservation projects, among others. There are approximately 476 million indigenous peoples, which constitute about 6 per cent of the global population. Indigenous territories cover roughly 22 per cent of the planet's land surface and harbour 80 per cent of its biodiversity. Indigenous peoples are the original guardians of our earth. The world must learn from their wisdom. Reason and justice dictate that in southern Nicobar, we should support and empower the islanders to continue to steward their ancestral territories, rather than robbing them of their lands, resources, lifeways and world views.

(First published as 'Empower the guardians of the earth, do not rob them', in *The Hindu*, 22 April 2024.)

7

A Threat to Indigenous Languages

Ajay Saini and Anvita Abbi

India's $9 billion megaproject on Great Nicobar, which includes a port, airport, power plant and township, aims to transform this remote island into a 'global destination for business, trade, and leisure'. Promoted as a 'holistic development' initiative in the peripheral Union Territory of the Andaman and Nicobar Islands, the project is set to cover 166.10 square kilometres in the first phase of the island's approximately 920 square kilometres area, nearly 850 square kilometres of which is a tribal reserve.

A UNESCO biosphere reserve, Great Nicobar is a tropical haven teeming with rare, endangered and endemic species of flora and fauna. The island is also home to two historically isolated indigenous communities—the Nicobarese and the Shompen, the latter categorised as a particularly vulnerable tribal group—whose millennia-old existence is deeply intertwined with the island's ecosystems.

Located in one of India's most seismically active zones, the megaproject threatens not only the island's fragile ecosystems and vulnerable indigenous communities but also puts the massive investment itself at great risk. While experts from various fields have highlighted the megaproject's numerous dangers, one critical aspect remains glaringly ignored—its catastrophic impact on indigenous languages.

How will this megaproject hasten the extinction of the Shompen and Nicobarese languages? What cultural and emotional toll will this loss exact on their speakers? And as these indigenous languages disappear, what irreplaceable knowledge, traditions and world views will be lost forever? These questions demand urgent attention.

The world speaks roughly 7,164 languages, but by the end of the century, 50–95 per cent could be extinct or critically endangered, with the indigenous languages facing the greatest risk. India, known for its linguistic diversity, is home to over 700 indigenous communities, which contribute immensely to this rich linguistic landscape. Alarmingly, around 156 languages spoken by fewer than 10,000 people are already endangered or on the brink of extinction.

One of the leading causes of language extinction in India is development-induced displacement, which has uprooted nearly 50 million people since Independence. Indigenous communities have borne a disproportionate share of this burden—despite making up only 8.6 per cent of the population in 2011, they account for over 40 per cent of those displaced by development projects.

Ironically, the timing of the megaproject is particularly striking. It coincided with the United Nations's launch of the International Decade of Indigenous Languages (2022–2032), which aims to raise awareness about the fragile state of indigenous languages and mobilise efforts for their preservation and revitalisation; and the adoption of the Kunming-Montreal Global Biodiversity

Framework (2022), a global blueprint for conserving, protecting, restoring, and sustainably managing biodiversity and ecosystems. Yet, India's actions in Great Nicobar stand in stark contradiction to these global commitments.

Before unveiling the project, the Indian government sought stakeholder views on potential tourism development in Great Nicobar. Both the Shompen and Nicobarese communities opposed the idea, urging the government to respect their habitat rights and ways of life. Despite their resistance, India chose to forge ahead with the megaproject.

The Shompen, a semi-nomadic, hunter-gatherer community of around 245 people, rely on the island's forest and riparian ecosystems for sustenance—ecosystems now under threat from the megaproject. The Nicobarese, once spread across the island's western, southwestern and southeastern coasts, practised a subsistence economy based on hunting, gathering, pig and poultry rearing, and the cultivation of coconut and areca nut.

Following the 2004 tsunami, the government relocated them to Campbell Bay, the island's administrative headquarters, as part of rescue and relief efforts, ultimately settling them there permanently against their will. For over two decades, the Nicobarese have repeatedly petitioned the government to return them to their ancestral lands, but their pleas have been denied.

For the Nicobarese and the Shompen, displacement from their ancestral lands is not merely a geographical or physical upheaval, it is a cognitive and cultural rupture. Their oral traditions, environmental knowledge and linguistic heritage are deeply intertwined with their land, forests and seascapes. Permanent displacement would push them into unfamiliar environments and linguistic settings, shattering the delicate balance between language, culture and ecology. The result? A rupture in intergenerational knowledge transfer, severing them from centuries of ecological wisdom, spiritual beliefs and survival strategies. Once cut off from their traditional habitats, their languages—and the vast knowledge they encode—stand on the brink of extinction.

The fate awaiting the Nicobarese and the Shompen finds a haunting parallel in the life of Boa Sr, the last speaker of the Great Andamanese language Bo. Displaced from Mayabunder in North Andaman to Strait Island in 1969-70, she spent her remaining years mourning the loss of her language and the ecological knowledge woven into it. Struggling to adapt to an unfamiliar landscape, she felt like an alien in a world she could no longer recognise, weighed down by isolation and depression until her passing in January 2010.

Boa was often seen speaking to birds, believing they were the only ones who understood her language. She told us that, according to Great Andamanese legend, their ancestors had transformed into birds—a belief that explains why this hunter-gatherer society never hunted birds. Other displaced members of the Great Andamanese communities likened their ancestral language to 'a corpse hanging from a tree'—a haunting image of a culture severed from its roots, stripped of life and meaning.

When a language disappears, it is not just words that are lost—entire ways of thinking, perceiving and interacting with the world vanish. The Shompen and Nicobarese languages encode millennia of ecological wisdom, from medicinal plants to survival strategies, woven into a world view where nature is not a resource to be exploited but an extension of identity. Displace these people, and their language fades. Erase their language, and an entire way of seeing the world is extinguished. The death of a language is the death of a world.

Language, ecology and culture are inseparable—displacing the indigenous people from their natural habitat unravels their identity, erodes their linguistic and cultural heritage, and pushes them towards extinction. The Great Nicobar megaproject is not just an ecological catastrophe; it is a deliberate, egregious act of linguistic and cultural genocide, masquerading as development.

India calls itself a republic, but that constitutional claim rings hollow if it fails to protect its diverse languages, cultures and peoples. A true republic does not abandon its indigenous tongues—it nurtures them, recognising that each lost language is a world erased.

(First published as 'India's $9bn Great Nicobar Megaproject Threatens Indigenous Languages', in *Earth Island Journal*, 19 February 2025.)

8

A Violation of Laws, a Threat to Rights

PANKAJ SEKHSARIA

There has been a fresh legal challenge to the controversial Great Nicobar Island project. The Rs 72,000 crore infrastructure project could spell devastation for the ecologically fragile region inhabited by the Shompen, a vulnerable indigenous group with a population of only about 250.

A petition filed in the Calcutta High Court in December 2024 has highlighted glaring violations of the Forest Rights Act in the clearances granted to the megaproject. The petition was filed by Meena Gupta, a former Secretary of Tribal Affairs and also Environment and Forests.

Crucially, the petition alleges that the recognition of forest rights certificate is void. It is the primary document under the Forest Rights Act allowing the project to go ahead. This means that the large forest area of the tribal communities on Great Nicobar cannot be diverted for use by the project.

The Petition

On 18 December, a bench of Chief Justice T.S. Sivagnanam and Justice Hiranmay Chatterjee admitted the petition and, in their order, noted the concerns listed by the petitioner. In the second hearing on 16 January, the respondents were given five more weeks to file their responses with the next hearing scheduled for 20 February.

The respondents include the Ministry of Environment, Forest and Climate Change, the Ministry of Tribal Affairs, the administration of the Andaman and Nicobar Islands, and the project proponent, the Andaman and Nicobar Islands Integrated Development Corporation Ltd (ANIIDCO).

The other respondents are Deputy Commissioner of Nicobar district and local bodies, such as the subdivisional-level committee for Great Nicobar constituted under the Forest Rights Act, the Directorate of Tribal Welfare, the Gram Panchayat of Laxminagar, Great Nicobar Island, all of whom are involved in facilitating the diversion of the forest for the project.

Mega Infrastructure Project

The Port Blair–based ANIIDCO is implementing the project which has four main components: a transshipment port at Galathea Bay, a greenfield airport, a power plant, and a greenfield township and tourism project. Great Nicobar Island is home to the Nicobarese community, a scheduled tribe, and the Shompen, a particularly vulnerable tribal group.

The massive project covers a total of 166 square kilometres of land, of which 130.75 square kilometres is forest area, which will be diverted for infrastructure development. Eighty-four square kilometres of the project land, some overlapping with the forest, is designated as a tribal reserve under the provisions of the Andaman and Nicobar Protection of Aboriginal Tribes, 1956. This, too, is sought to be denotified for the project. In a letter dated 12 August 2021, the tribal welfare department of the Andaman and Nicobar administration assured the project proponent that it 'will seek required exemptions' from regulations to protect tribal and forest dwellers 'as may be needed for the project'.

Stage 1 forest clearance, to divert the forest land, was granted by the Ministry of Environment, Forest and Climate Change in October 2022 and was followed by Environment and Coastal Regulation Zone clearance a month later, in November. Condition number 26 of the forest clearance had explicitly asked for compliance with the Forest Rights Act before the forest could be diverted for the project.

Multiple FRA Violations

The petition argues that there are multiple violations of the Forest Rights Act as well as the Ministry of Environment's 3 August 2009 order, which mandates that state governments strictly comply with the Act and settlement of forest rights before diversion of forest lands. Central to the petition's contention is the recognition of the forest rights certificate issued by the Deputy Commissioner of Nicobar on 18 August 2022.

It states that all processes for settlement of rights under the Forest Rights Act have been carried out for the diversion of 130 square kilometres of forest land and that the rights of the particularly vulnerable tribal group have been protected. This certificate is the primary document under the Forest Rights Act allowing the project to go ahead.

This certificate, the petition contends, is null and void on several grounds. One of the key violations is the constitution of the subdivisional-level committee for Great Nicobar constituted under the Forest Rights Act. According to Section 5(c) of the Forest Rights Rules, the subdivisional-level committee should have at least two members of a Scheduled Tribe, but in this case, there was only one member of the Nicobarese community.

A fourth member, in the form of the Tribal Welfare Officer of the Andaman Adim Janjati Vikas Samiti, was nominated and authorised to give consent on behalf of the Shompen. The petition notes that there is no provision under the Forest Rights Act for someone to represent a particularly vulnerable tribal group, leave alone give consent on their behalf.

There is also a prominent conflict of interest: the project proponent ANIIDCO and the Andaman Adim Janjati Vikas Samiti are both under the same leadership—the Andaman and Nicobar Island administration. The grant of this certificate also conflicts with the reports submitted by the local administration to the Ministry of Tribal Affairs for the years 2018–24 showing that no claims were settled under the Forest Rights Act.

The gram sabha of Laxminagar Panchayat that finally approved the diversion, the petition notes, is 'not the gram sabha under section 2(g) of FRA'. The gram sabha had no members of either the Scheduled Tribe or the particularly vulnerable tribal group community and has no validity or authority under the Forest Rights Act.

Long Delay

Raising questions of process and intention, the petition notes that while the Forest Rights Act was notified in 2007, it took more than fourteen years and six months to constitute the mandated subdivisional-level committee for grant of rights to the tribal communities in Great Nicobar.

Yet, it took just twenty-three days between the constitution of the subdivisional-level committee on 26 July 2022 and the recognition of forest rights certificate being issued on 18 August 2022 through a process where the communities themselves had no role to play, which is a serious violation of their rights. The minutes of the subdivisional-level committee meeting are further vitiated by the fact that the proceedings are signed by E.S. Rajesh, a local contractor, businessman and a political functionary who should not have been even present there.

Given that the project is being pushed despite the violation of multiple laws such as the Forest Rights Act, 2006, Forest Conservation Act, 1980 and the Right to Fair Compensation and Transparency in Land Acquisition, Rehabilitation and Resettlement Act, 2013, the outcome of the petition will have an important bearing on the conservation of these ancient forests and rights of the Shompen and Nicobarese who have been living here for thousands of years.

(First published as 'Great Nicobar Island Project Violates Several Laws, Rights of Shompen: Petition in Calcutta HC', in *Scroll.in*, 10 February 2025.)

TWO DECADES AFTER A TSUNAMI

9

20 Christmases After the Tsunami

LEESHA K. NAIR

'YÔNTĪ An ngam Yöng Tēv, aṅ el haliöngö,
Hëtö finötnyi, Yöng töm Töhet Rēlö;
Ngam Yöng tö-örheūheu-aṅ, Anga-aṅ Yöng,
Haròh el chūökkuö nuā, el kantēra Mā;
Tā-a, töi ha-öiny ngam hanāngenlōn Ò,
Tön yônti An nö hayööken tökööl hī.'

The hymn echoed through the Nicobarese settlement of Rajiv Nagar in Great Nicobar, weaving its way through structures that its residents now call home, illuminated by strings of bright, festive lights. Yet, amidst the celebration of Christmas, a deep sense of longing permeated the air—nostalgia for a way of life that the 2004 Indian Ocean tsunami had all but erased.

'Christmas back then meant travelling for days between villages to celebrate with everyone. We carried heavy loads but were happy. Now, we are cramped in one place. This doesn't feel like the Christmas we knew before the waves came,' said Robert,[1] leading the carolers past tin shelters that still don't feel like home, even twenty years later.

The Devouring Sea

On that fateful day, 26 December 2004, the sea rose as an unholy leviathan. Nine carollers, journeying to their villages along western Great Nicobar Island, were the sole survivors along that coast. What awaited them was ruin beyond comprehension. The western shores of Great Nicobar—once alive with the vibrancy of life, songs and sacred rituals—had been devoured in a single, merciless moment. Entire villages had vanished beneath the waves, leaving behind no trace of their forms. For the nine survivors, there was no solace, only an aching void where their kin, their homes and their way of life had once thrived.

The 2004 Indian Ocean tsunami was no mere calamity; it was a reckoning. An estimated 2,28,000 lives were lost across fifteen countries, with Indonesia, Sri Lanka, India, the Maldives and Thailand bearing the brunt of the destruction. Great Nicobar Island, lying perilously close to the epicentre, Indonesia's Banda Aceh, suffered immensely. Across the Nicobar Islands, 7,330 were counted among the dead—with another 5,900 still missing to this day.

The aftermath was a tragedy of another kind—one crafted by human hands. By mid-2005, the Nicobarese survivors, still reeling from the devastation, were uprooted from their ancestral villages on the western coasts of Great Nicobar Island, and cast across the island's eastern side into hastily constructed tin shelters in Rajiv Nagar and New Chingenh. The discomfort stretched on, and by the 2010s, 'permanent shelters' appeared—towering structures of iron girders and wooden planks, some perched precariously on stilts.

'The government's involvement with the Nicobarese was very minimal. They never interfered, but were rather facilitators. The Nicobarese conducted themselves on their own terms. Post-tsunami, the government made decisions for them. The housing options provided to the community were not in cognizance of how the Nicobarese organised themselves; they were for nuclear families rather than joint families,' a senior social anthropologist who has worked with the Nicobarese for two decades told *The Diplomat* on the condition of anonymity.

Now, twenty years have passed, and the Nicobarese continue to plead for the return to their ancestral lands; lands that hold not just their memories, but their very identity and way of life. Today, around 500 Great Nicobarese, the smallest community of Nicobarese in the world, live crammed into these settlements which continue to be alien to them.

Life at Higher Ground

'I really don't know how to maintain this place,' said Joseph. 'The room becomes unbearably hot during summers, and during the rains, the roofs leak. When cyclonic weather strikes, we men are up all night, draining water from the lower floors. There have been nights I haven't slept, endlessly scooping out water. If these homes were made of wood, we would know how to repair or maintain them. But if we have to repair these metal structures, it would cost us extensively. We can't afford it.'

Before the waves reshaped their world, Nicobari villages thrived on a deeply rooted system of kinship and communal harmony. Resources weren't individually owned but collectively shared within these close-knit groups. Elders were revered as reservoirs of traditional knowledge. The division of labour, though flexible, followed a natural rhythm. Men ventured into the forests, plantations and the sea, bringing back food from the land and water. Women, on the other hand, wielded power as decision-makers, overseeing every stage of resource management, from sourcing to processing. Now, stripped of their traditional responsibilities, they've been thrust into roles that were never theirs to shoulder.

'I don't like to see my daughters working as manual labourers for someone else,' said Cynthia, a mother of three. 'It is something we have never done. But what can I do? We have to survive. We women have extra expenses compared to men. If we go back to our old villages, we won't have to worry about feeding the family. Here, that is the main worry. That's why we also have to work.'

The rehabilitation efforts, while well-intentioned, were blind to the nuances of Nicobarese life. Relocating them from the coasts severed old connections and disrupted their cultural backbone. The tsunami took with it a significant portion of the elder population, and with them went the deep-rooted knowledge of their traditions. Now, an entire generation is growing up oblivious to the ways of their ancestors, leaving the surviving elders concerned about their vanishing heritage.

Take, for instance, the role of pigs in their culture. These animals were integral to their festivities, a symbol of community and celebration. In their old villages, the pigs thrived, foraging freely across the land. But the cramped, sterile settlements in Rajiv Nagar have no space for such animals to roam. The pig population has dwindled, reducing the number of festivals the tribe can celebrate. What was once a cornerstone of their culture has now become a rarity. What is the equivalent to gold among the Nicobarese is often seen as a menace by the non-tribal communities nearby.

Conflict with Non-Tribals

The relocated Nicobarese, once nestled in the isolation of their ancestral villages, now find themselves in unavoidable proximity to non-tribals, primarily Telugu settlers whose tsunami rehabilitation settlement lies just a stone's throw away. With this forced mingling has come an unrelenting erosion of their privacy.

Recently, a bold message appeared on a signboard erected by the Nicobarese at the entrance of a road connecting the two settlements: '24×7 Non-Tribals, Not Allowed.' The sign stands like a silent sentinel, a desperate attempt to reclaim boundaries that are repeatedly trespassed. Yet, despite this assertion of autonomy, their spaces remain intruded upon. 'If they want something from us, they can call us outside,' said Suman, a Nicobarese teenager, her frustration barely contained. 'But they always want to enter using some excuse.'

Campbell Bay, a microcosm of India's diversity, is home to settlers from Punjab, Tamil Nadu, Andhra Pradesh, Kerala and many other states. In the 1970s, families of retired military personnel were resettled here by the government, followed by other mainlanders in search of better livelihoods. Adding to the mosaic are defence personnel stationed on the islands, creating a mixed but uneasy cohabitation.

In the early days after their relocation, the Nicobarese were acutely made aware of their 'otherness'. Despite being the original inhabitants of the islands, they were made to feel inferior to their settler counterparts. Their distinct Mongoloid features became an easy target for ridicule. They struggled to speak Hindi fluently, a fact that was not only mocked but wielded as a weapon to belittle them. Their children, too, bore the brunt, criticised in schools for being 'slower' than settler kids.

'Our kids now give it back to them. They don't hold back anymore,' said Cleo, a Nicobarese woman, as she meticulously stitched a new blouse in preparation for Christmas. 'We used to hesitate to talk to the settlers back then because we didn't know Hindi. And that's what they'd always ask us—"Why don't you know Hindi?" Why would I speak Hindi to my people? They wouldn't understand much! Even now, many of us don't speak the language. My Hindi is still weak,' she laughed.

The tension extends beyond language and schools into the physical spaces of their lives. The Nicobarese ancestral plantations, rich with areca nuts and coconuts, are regularly exploited by the settlers, harvesting its bounty without consent or consideration.

'When we go back, we see our old plantations without much produce,' said Robert, his tone a mix of resignation and anger. 'If they want to take, they can take—but leave something for us. They don't just take; they ruin the plantations by excessive chopping, leaving the waste scattered everywhere. By the time we go back to harvest, there is nothing left for us.'

A New Catastrophe

As the Nicobarese continue to grapple with coexisting alongside non-tribals, a storm of greater magnitude brews on the horizon. The Indian government's ambitious plans to develop the islands have brought with them the spectre of displacement, ecological destruction and cultural obliteration.

The Great Nicobar Project, a Rs 720 billion (around $9 billion) venture has drawn global attention for all the wrong reasons. Dismissed by many as an ecological catastrophe in the making, the project has been branded as a death sentence for the Shompens, one of the last indigenous tribes of the islands. For the government, however, it is a jewel in India's strategic crown: a plan to dominate the Malacca Strait, the world's busiest sea route.

To achieve this vision, the government intends to divert 130 square kilometres of pristine rainforest—an expanse larger than many small towns. Of this, 84 square kilometres lie within tribal reserves, sacred lands that have sustained indigenous communities for generations. The feasibility study for this colossal undertaking, conducted by the consulting firm AECOM for NITI Aayog in March 2021, suggests constructing an international port, an airport, a power plant, a township and tourism infrastructure—all on what the report claims is 'uninhabited' land.

In 2022, during discussions for environmental clearance, an Expert Appraisal Committee (EAC) asserted that the project would not disturb the Nicobarese or the Shompens. To keep these indigenous peoples away from the thousands of workers and settlers who will flood the island, the draft Environmental Impact Assessment (EIA) even proposed erecting barbed wire fences.

Yet, the promises that the Great Nicobar Project will proceed with sensitivity are already unravelling. To 'compensate' for the environmental destruction, the government announced the creation of three sanctuaries for displaced leatherback turtles, corals and Nicobar megapodes on Little Nicobar, Meroe and Menchal Islands. These islands, however, are ancestral lands of the Nicobarese. Shockingly, no consultation with the tribal communities took place.

Barnabas Manju, the Chairman of the Tribal Council for Great Nicobar and Little Nicobar, stumbled upon the notification of these sanctuaries during a routine visit to the Assistant Commissioner's office. 'I saw the notice about the sanctuaries on the board when I went to the AC office. We were not consulted about it, nor were we given a copy of the notice,' he said, disbelief evident in his voice.

In August 2022, the Tribal Council took the first steps to resist this forced decision. They penned a letter to the Deputy Commissioner of Nicobar District, with copies sent to the Chief Secretary, lieutenant Governor and forest officials. Yet their plea was met with silence—an overwhelming, deafening refusal to engage. Instead, the administration's final blow to their concerns was issuing official notifications to create the three wildlife sanctuaries just two months later—the decision again devoid of dialogue or consent.

The tipping point came in November 2022 when the Tribal Council formally withdrew consent for the diversion of their reserved lands for the Great Nicobar Project. The letter revealed a disturbing truth: they had not been informed that parts of their pre-tsunami villages along the southeast and southwest coasts would also be denotified. This critical information had been deliberately concealed during public hearings, where assurances were given that their lands would remain untouched.

Old Fears, New Fears

'The tsunami took everything from us in one go, but this new project will take what remains with us bit by bit,' said Robert, his voice heavy with both frustration and resignation. 'I also fear the tsunami returning, especially during Christmas. The Shompens fear it even more than we do. What if it comes back again? My son is studying outside the islands. What if it happens when he's not here? I was his age—just seventeen—when the tsunami happened. I lost everything. I don't want him to have the same fate.'

For the Nicobarese, the solution to their plight is clear: They want to return to their ancestral villages, but they are pragmatic too. They understand that an abrupt relocation would push them further into instability. What they seek is a gradual shift, one where their devastated villages, overtaken by debris and overgrowth, are cleared with the administration's help. Instead, they are met with vague assurances and bureaucratic indifference.

'They told us we'll go back when the road is constructed,' another Nicobarese resident, John, explained. 'The administration thinks tribals can live anywhere, but that is not how it works. If I can live anywhere, can I just go and live in their houses? No, right? We have our own way with forests and land, and we want to live that way.'

'We also fear that after moving our kids won't be able to attend schools. The officials said we won't be able to access hospitals if we go back. I have diabetes, a disease that I didn't even know about before coming here. What to do, our diet has changed,' said Janice, a Nicobari elder.

The government's neglect of the Nicobarese stands in stark contrast to its repeated proclamations of championing tribal rights. 'The welfare of tribal communities has been at the forefront of our policies. We launched the [Rs 240 billion] JanMan Yojana for the most backward tribal groups. Today, houses are being built for them, and roads are being constructed to connect them to the broader society,' declared Prime Minister Narendra Modi in November, while unveiling development projects worth over RS 66.4 billion aimed at uplifting tribal communities in Bihar. The Bharatiya Janata Party (BJP) has often emphasised its dedication to tribal welfare, proudly citing the election of Droupadi Murmu as India's first tribal president. And yet, the 'Ghar Wapasi'—the long-awaited homecoming of the Nicobarese—seems to have been forgotten amidst the fanfare.

'The best approach right now is to consult and participate with them, rather than dictating terms. All the administrators that have come after the tsunami have been dictators. In the past, there was engagement with the tribes, even though a minimal one. They don't need to be told what to do and what not to do, they'll figure that out themselves. They just need to be facilitated, that's all,' added the senior social anthropologist.

What began as a promise of refuge has now turned into a prolonged exile, leaving the Nicobarese stranded between a past they mourn and a present they cannot accept. Every Christmas, they celebrate with what little they have, but the joy is fleeting. As the night of celebration fades, they wake the next morning haunted by what was lost the day after Christmas in 2004—the people, the home, a way of life, and the sense of belonging to the land they once called their own.

(First published in *The Diplomat*, 27 December 2024.)

10

'The Death of Life'

Ajay Saini

Two decades ago, when the Indian Ocean tsunami wiped out their remote village of Pulobhabi on Great Nicobar's western coast, nine Nicobarese defied the odds and survived the deadly waves. Their lifeline? The forest—their oldest ally—sheltered, nourished and sustained them. For nearly six weeks, they relied entirely on its bounty, navigating its depths until they emerged on the island's eastern coast at Campbell Bay, where rescuers found them and brought them to relief camps.

The ancient forests of Great Nicobar—a UNESCO biosphere reserve and the ancestral home of the Nicobarese and Shompen, a particularly vulnerable tribal group—have sustained these historically isolated communities for millennia. Today, this lifeline faces an existential threat from a Rs 81,800 crore megaproject set to transform the island into a 'global destination of business, trade, and leisure'. Official estimates put the number of trees to be felled for the megaproject at about 1 million, but ecologists warn that the true toll could be as high as 10 million.

What does this loss of forest mean for Great Nicobar's indigenous people?

When I asked Mathias, one of the nine tsunami survivors from Pulobhabi—whose ancestral village now lies in the shadow of the megaproject—his answer cuts to the core: 'The death of life'.

His words foretell a catastrophe. To grasp its magnitude, we must ask: What is a forest to the people who call it home? Is it merely a resource, or do they share some deeper, inseparable bond with it? And when that bond is severed, what disappears forever?

Borne of a Bamboo Stem

My ethnographic research in the Nicobar has revealed the profound spiritual connection its indigenous inhabitants share with their lands, forests and ocean. To them, these are not just physical spaces but living entities, infused with spirits and inseparable from their way of life.

The forest is more than just trees. It is the foundation of their identity, the taproot of their vitality, and a sacred sanctuary where the social, natural and divine realms converge. Above all, it is family. This bond is embedded in their cosmology and creation stories, shaping their way of life for generations.

One such creation story from Great Nicobar tells of a time when the island lay uninhabited, until a boy descended from the sky and vanished deep into the earth. Days later, a lemon shoot emerged, growing into a towering tree heavy with flowers and fruit. From the lemon seeds of its northern branches sprang the ancestors of the Kondul, Teressa, Trinket and Nancowry islanders, while the seeds of its southern branches gave rise to the people of Great Nicobar. Over time, however, a rift grew between them—a divergence in thought and way of life. One group, now known as the Shompen, retreated deep into the jungle. The other, the Nicobarese, settled along the coasts.

This story is more than just a tale of origin. The lemon tree, with its roots anchored in the earth and its branches reaching skyward, symbolises the people's shared identity and enduring bond with nature. It serves as a reminder that the survival of these indigenous communities is intricately linked to the forests and land that have sustained them for generations.

A similar folktale from Car Nicobar tells of a great deluge that drowned all but one man, who survived by climbing the tallest tree. When the waters receded, he spotted a lone bitch perched on another tree and took her as his wife. From their union, the island was repopulated. Though mythical, the tale carries a deeper truth: the interconnectedness of humans, animals and trees.

This kinship with nature is not unique to the Nicobarese. Several indigenous societies share deep connections with the flora and fauna of their homelands. The Popol Vuh, the sacred text of the K'iche' Maya (indigenous people of the Americas), narrates how the gods created humans from maize, the region's staple food. To the K'iche' people, animals are not just wild creatures but neighbours with agency. Through stories such as these, the Popol Vuh offers a window into pre-Columbian Mesoamerica, where nature and humanity were inseparably woven together.

Similarly, the Great Andamanese trace their lineage to bamboo. They believe that Phertajido—the first man of the Andamans—was born from the hollow of a bamboo stem. For them, birds are not merely creatures of the sky but the reincarnated spirits of their ancestors. So deeply held is this belief that hunting birds is unthinkable.

Andamans, Replayed

For indigenous communities, the forest is more than a home or a source of sustenance: it is a realm of reverence, reciprocity and deep belonging. The forest is not a resource to be plundered; it is an ancestral guardian that nurtures and protects. And in return, it must be honoured and safeguarded.

Indigenous communities have waged spirited battles to protect their forests and commons, often at great personal cost. The Chipko Andolan, the Narmada Bachao Andolan, the Jungle Bachao Andolan, the Niyamgiri movement, the Hasdeo Arand resistance, the Nyishi and Adi opposition to dams, and movements against palm oil plantations and deforestation in northeast India are among the many historical and ongoing indigenous struggles.

Some of their struggles, however, have remained largely unknown. For instance, when the British colonised the Andaman Islands in the nineteenth century and began clearing forests to establish a penal colony, the Great Andamanese did not stand by as their homeland was destroyed. Armed with little more than bows and arrows, they waged a fierce resistance against the mightiest empire—but at a terrible cost. Ruthless massacres and foreign diseases brought them to the brink of extinction.

After India became independent, this destruction only intensified. Ancient tropical forests were cleared for infrastructure projects and the resettlement of mainland settlers. The Jarawas, who had long defended their ancestral lands, fiercely resisted this encroachment. Their defiance, however, came at a tragic cost—many were electrocuted while opposing the Andaman Trunk Road, a project that cut through their forests, scarring not just the land but their very existence.

Such indigenous resistance is more than a fight for land, forests or resources; it is an assertion of identity, a stand against erasure.

For indigenous peoples, the forest is not just essential to life; it is life itself—breathing through their way of living, enduring in their memories and flowing through their traditions. To sever this bond is to unravel the very fabric of their existence. The loss of the forest is not merely an ecological catastrophe; it is the annihilation of a people's history, culture and way of being.

Ironically, the champions of the Great Nicobar megaproject refuse to learn from history: the destruction of both forests and indigenous people of the Andamans. Instead, they seem determined to repeat it in Nicobar.

The Vigilant Black Stone

Indigenous people have long been at the forefront of protecting the earth. Though they comprise just 6 per cent of the global population—about 476 million people—their territories span nearly 22 per cent of the planet's land surface and sustain 80 per cent of its biodiversity. Their knowledge and practices, honed over generations, are vital to preserving fragile ecosystems.

For centuries, the Nicobarese have safeguarded Great Nicobar's ecosystems, guided by the belief that all beings—living and non-living—possess spirit and agency. This world view is not merely an abstract idea but a way of life, shaping their relationship with nature.

During my fieldwork in Little Nicobar, I went fishing with my Nicobarese friend, Gilbert. Using only a hook and line, he spent hours catching just a few fish. Curious, I asked why he didn't use a small-eye net. 'If we use a net, we will catch plenty of fish in no time, more than we need. Some will surely go to waste. And the god of the ocean will not be pleased with that,' he replied. In an ocean teeming with fish—where they grow old and die, often untouched—his words offer an invaluable lesson in sustainable management.

The Nicobarese culture is rich with practices and taboos that have safeguarded nature for generations. Take, for instance, chat-mat—a tree in the forests of Great Nicobar, believed to house a spirit. To harm it—by cutting its limbs or wounding its bark—is to invite a curse: swollen eyes and a body covered in eruptions like chickenpox. For the Nicobarese, this is not mere superstition but a sacred covenant with the forest—a reminder that it is alive, pulsing with spirits that watch over all who dwell within it.

Similarly, Great Nicobar's forests hold an enigmatic black stone, tirah, that lies in silent vigilance—believed to be alive. To disturb its peace—by shouting, cutting wood or showing any sign of disrespect—is to invite grave consequences: a raging fever, blood vomiting, even death. This belief is not merely rooted in fear but in a deep understanding of the interconnectedness of all things—where even a stone holds power, purpose and a place in the sacred balance of life.

Beyond the forests, in the restless waters of the sea, another creature commands deep reverence: the hiput, dugong. To spear a hiput is to shatter the harmony of the elements, unleashing chaos. The sea itself is believed to mourn the loss, its grief manifesting in violent storms and cyclones (labifui), punishing those who dare spill the blood of an innocent creature.

Even entire islands in Nicobar are imbued with spiritual significance and fiercely protected by the Nicobarese. Menchal and Meroë Islands—known to them as Pingaeyak and Piruii—are officially recorded as uninhabited in government documents. Yet, for the Nicobarese of Great and Little Nicobar, these islands are vital lifelines, serving as crucial resource repositories over which they hold traditional rights.

Menchal, or Pingaeyak, is believed to be the dwelling place of a powerful spirit that watches over the island. For the Nicobarese, it is not merely an island but a sacred realm, alive with forces that demand reverence and care. Similarly, Meroë, or Piruii, is steeped in legend, said to be home to a mythical islander community. The protection of these islands is enshrined in spiritual belief systems and upheld through age-old practices of sustainable natural resource management, ensuring their sanctity remains untouched.

In the Nicobarese world view, the social, natural and spiritual realms are inseparable, reflecting a deep connection to nature—one rooted not in ownership, but in stewardship. In a world increasingly driven by exploitation, Great Nicobar offers a profound lesson: some places are not meant to be conquered or commodified but cherished and preserved.

Where Trees Once Roamed

To the Nicobarese, nature is not to be tamed or exploited. As a sentient, interconnected being, it listens, watches and responds. This belief lies at the heart of their world view, shaping a code of ethics—an ecological wisdom passed down through generations. To harm the forest, land or sea is not merely an act of destruction; it is an act of defiance against the very forces that sustain life. And what happens when these forces are defied? A Nicobarese folktale offers a telling answer: Long ago, trees were not bound to the earth—they roamed freely, heeding the commands of humans. People harnessed them as living vehicles, tying bundles of goods to their branches and guiding them from the jungle to their villages. Some even rode upon their sturdy limbs.

But one day, as the trees carried the heavy loads, they swayed and bumped into one another. Amused, the people laughed mockingly, wounding the trees' pride. Angered, the trees refused to take another step. From that day on, they stood still, leaving humans to bear their own burdens—forever reminded of the nurturing bond they once shared with trees and the cost of taking it for granted.

As the spectre of the megaproject looms over the Great Nicobar, we must ask: What dies when a forest falls? What does felling 10 million trees in an ancient tropical forest mean for India? The answer lies in the lessons we refuse to learn—the storms we summon, the fragile ecological balance we shatter—all in the name of development. Climate change, droughts, floods, landslides, species extinction—each a cost of our recklessness—is already upon us.

The Great Nicobar megaproject isn't just a local catastrophe; it's a national crisis. It threatens to erase one of India's last great biodiversity hotspots, obliterate carbon sinks that shield us from climate chaos, and sever the sacred bond between indigenous communities and nature.

Progress built on nature's ruins isn't progress; it's a reckless gamble with the future. And it's one we can no longer afford.

(First published in *Frontline*, 25 March 2025.)

FRAGILE ECOLOGIES

11

An Obit for Patai Takaru

ROHAN ARTHUR AND T.R. SHANKAR RAMAN

Trofim Lysenko was a radical plant biologist of the Soviet era. He was convinced that rational science should be used in the service of the state, and that the purpose of the state was progress for all, and at all costs. Lysenko was convinced that his knowledge of plant inheritance could be deployed to feed the revolution. Rejecting bourgeois phantoms like the gene as just so much metaphysics designed to maintain class structures, he believed that crops, much like ideal Soviet citizens, could bend to the will of the state, with just the right environment and training. Within a few generations of careful Lamarckian engineering, any crop could become highly productive, helping fill vacant granaries across the republic.

It was a beautiful, transformative idea. Lysenkoism shaped official agricultural policy in the Soviet republic from the 1930s until the early 1950s, setting crop production targets for farmer collectives, who were directed to use its principles of 'vernalisation' and vegetative hybridisation to double their yields. Farms unable to meet these targets were clearly tilled by unpatriotic or lazy farmers, unconvinced of the grand revolutionary project. Intellectual doubters were jailed or executed. Declining yields and near famines were not enough to shake Lysenkoism's grip over the nation, and it spread to other socialist regimes, including China, where it contributed to the many devastations of the Great Leap Forward.

It is not important here to retell the sorry saga of Lysenkoism since enough has been written about it earlier.[1] Yet, it is a sobering example of how a beautiful idea can capture, transform and bring a nation to its knees. Lysenkoism was not merely a beautiful idea, of course. It was an ambitious ideology based on enlightenment thinking. It was an audacious experiment in ecological and social engineering. It was, eventually, an instrument of state making. And it had the misfortune of being almost wholly wrong.

But if misconceived ideas inevitably lead to ruin, well-conceived ones, misapplied, can do the same. Ecological restoration, the hopeful idea that we can reverse the trajectory of degrading habitats with careful ecological engineering, is one such. Unlike Lysenkoism, it has its intellectual foundations in sound principles of ecological theory. Under the right circumstances, and when done right, it has a proven track record of succeeding. It may be among our best chances of recouping losses in formerly disturbed or damaged natural ecosystems. Yet, when made to work in the service of an essentially ill-thought scheme, it becomes yet another disingenuous instrument of state making.

Consider India's plans for the island of Great Nicobar in the Indian Ocean. A major transshipment terminal together with an international airport and a brand new city are set to transform the region, dragging it into a world of untapped economic opportunity.

The Union government's plans for Great Nicobar, estimated to cost Rs 72,000 crore (recently revised upwards to more than Rs 81,800 crore), include a new port (for container transshipment), a new international airport, an entire new city and a power plant.

The 'pre-feasibility' report prepared by AECOM India Pvt. Ltd, a Haryana-based consultancy, for the Union's think tank NITI Aayog indicated that 'tourism facilities (hotels, resorts, dining, shopping, and entertainment) are to be developed within the urban centres up and down the coast'. Making all this a reality requires the bulldozing of large tracts of primary rainforest. The construction activity will have large and permanent impacts on coastal and marine systems. Local communities, including indigenous Nicobarese, will either be displaced or have their lands significantly modified.

Several incisive articles have critically examined the proposed development and drawn attention to the drastic impacts on ecology[2] and social justice,[3] while raising questions on whether the projects are even economically viable[4] or geopolitically necessary[5] at all. Our purpose in this article is not to revisit or reiterate these aspects; instead, we examine, in the context of ecological impact, how the idea of restoration is being deployed to compensate for the planned destruction of forest and marine habitats.

The project proponents claim that all ecological impacts will be addressed with ambitious plans to offset the damage. Lost rainforest will be compensated with afforestation efforts elsewhere in India, and entire reefs will be salvaged and relocated safely away from the path of the planned destruction. It is our submission that, as marvellous as these measures may sound, they constitute a plan that rivals Lysenkoism in its inspired ecological hubris and represent a worrying trend in the developmental logic of the country.

Great Nicobar is the largest and southernmost island among the Nicobars of the Andaman and Nicobar archipelago. The Nicobars are the only region within India to fall within the Sundaland global biodiversity hotspot, a recognition of its extraordinary biological richness, including numerous endemic specie such as the rare Nicobar megapode, Nicobar tree shrew, cat snakes, tree frog and plants. One in three bird species and one in four plant species of Great Nicobar are found nowhere else in the world. The island remains clothed in dense forests from coastal mangroves to evergreen rainforests, and scientists continue to discover and describe new species with nearly every expedition. Below water too, this region borders the great Coral Triangle, home to more than 75 per cent of the world's coral species and to an astounding diversity of fish and marine invertebrates.

To the Great Nicobarese people, the island's original inhabitants, the island is Patai Takaru, or 'big island'. The Nicobarese have long lived alongside another indigenous community, the semi-nomadic and forest-dwelling Shompen, a particularly vulnerable tribal group numbering perhaps around 250 people. It is under the traditional ownership and conservation of these tribal communities that the island's extraordinary forests and biological diversity have survived to the present day. While scientists and conservationists have raised the alarm at the impending ecological catastrophe about to befall the island, social scientists and human rights groups have warned against the impending human tragedy or 'genocide' of the indigenes if the plans go through.

'Restoring' Rainforests, Relocating Reefs

The Environmental Impact Assessment (EIA) for the Great Nicobar project, carried out by Vimta Labs, concluded in March 2022. The environmental clearance granted in November 2022 mentioned several mitigation measures, including the creation of a leatherback turtle sanctuary on Little Nicobar, and a suite of measures to restore or compensate for lost rainforests and coral reefs. The project will destroy an estimated 13,075 hectares of pristine tropical rainforest, including 8,52,245 trees within the Great Nicobar Biosphere Reserve. This estimate is likely an underestimate as it relies on a limited survey by a consultant with no direct expertise in the Nicobars. A highly conservative extrapolation of rigorous tree density estimates done in 2003 by three leading Indian primatologists indicates that the true number of trees affected could be closer to 40 lakh trees (4 million), five times higher than the official figure.[6, 7] Of course, there is no way to be certain of the estimate until the details are released transparently, including maps of the area where tree-felling will be carried out, number of plots surveyed, plot sizes and tree girths considered, and the results of enumeration.[8]

The government has proposed 'green development' for some areas, reserving 15 per cent as green and open spaces, but such interventions are incompatible with the preservation of dense rainforests. The EIA fails to account for the broader ecological impacts, including soil erosion and the loss of unique ecosystems like giant tree fern forests. Nor does it consider other serious environmental harms such as large-scale soil erosion during logging affecting terrestrial, riverine and marine ecosystems. It fails to recognise that deforestation of mature tropical rainforests can release as much as 650 tonnes of carbon dioxide per hectare, or over 4.3 million tonnes of CO_2 by deforesting 6,599 hectares, which is equivalent to burning over 1.6 billion litres of diesel.

Against these losses, a truly Lysenkoist plan is being offered as a remedy. To offset the loss of Patai Takaru's remarkable rainforests, the government plans to establish compensatory tree plantations in double the area in—rather unbelievably—the Aravallis of Haryana and a small part of Madhya Pradesh. The Haryana plans include the creation of a 10,000 acre 'zoo safari' park.[9] These plans ignore the fact that the Aravallis and central India are vastly different and drier ecosystems, with completely different forest types, ecologies, biogeography and evolutionary history.

It is difficult to imagine how this can be regarded as compensating for the loss of the Nicobar rainforests. Furthermore, compensatory afforestation plantations in India have an abysmal track record, marked by monoculture plantations, use of alien species, poor survival, and wastage of land and public resources, as flagged by a Comptroller and Auditor General report as early as 2013 and in many studies since.[10] [11]

Below water, although no coral was found in Galathea Bay itself, reefs on the eastern flank might be impacted by dredging, with an estimated loss of 1–2 hectares of reef from airport construction. To offset this, the report recommended relocating corals from 4 hectares of reef to Laxman and Joginder Nagar beaches. This translocation, managed by the Zoological Survey of India (ZSI), involves moving 16,150 coral colonies. Of these, around 6,900 of the identified colonies belong to the dominant genus Acropora, around 8,000 are massive or submassive colonies, and the rest an assortment of other groups. The proposal is to use saws, chisels and drills to hack corals off the substrate before transporting them in water to the new/recovery site, where they will be fixed with epoxy and monitored for survival. The salvage operation will cost Rs 55 crore, and will be monitored for a decade.

Ecological Restoration as a Conservation Strategy

Whether for coral reefs or for rainforests, it is useful to ask how legitimate these proposed solutions are. Given the rash of restoration efforts that abound, what do we know of their effectiveness? We will say upfront that, although we have been engaged with restoring rainforests and in coral reef conservation for the past twenty-five years, there are no straightforward answers. In this section, we briefly summarise the current state of knowledge of the restoration of rainforests and coral reefs in the hope that it will stimulate a reconsideration of the existing restoration proposals for Great Nicobar and help inform better mitigation measures.

Even if one assumes that the destroyed rainforests can be ecologically restored, how can one go about it and what are its chances of success? Within India, the Nicobars itself is biogeographically distinctive as part of the Sunda region and has generally excellent forest cover that is not in need of restorative interventions—they are best left alone. This itself indicates that there are virtually no opportunities for ecological restoration in the truest sense. In other words, if the forests are destroyed for this project on Great Nicobar, their loss will be complete, irreversible and irreplaceable. It is precisely for this reason that the first and cardinal rule of the ten golden rules for reforestation[12] states: Protect existing forest first.

Compared with the compensatory plan in the Aravallis, a somewhat more reasonable proposal for restoration could have targeted degraded areas in the Andaman Islands, on the logic of partial similarity with the Nicobars. This could have meant restoring areas such as the over 1,500 hectares of failed oil palm plantation in Little Andaman or the extensively logged forest areas on many of the Andaman Islands. However, at present, the government plans only to revive oil palm rather than restore forests, and there is no coherent approach or policy to revive degraded logged forests or tackle invasive alien species on the islands.[13] [14]

If ecological restoration is attempted, a spectrum of approaches can be used.[15] This ranges from relatively passive ones (allowing forests to regenerate naturally with protection), to assisted forest regeneration (with interventions such as removal of choking weeds or adding bird perches as loci of seed dispersal to promote regeneration), to active and reconstructive restoration (involving more intensive work such as soil amendments, weed removal, and reintroduction of a high diversity of native species with planting and site maintenance over many years).

The choice of the appropriate method for any given degraded site involves many considerations, including understanding the causes that led to the degradation, the sites' ecological history and land use, and the landscape context, geology and soils. It requires pinpointing the original natural vegetation types, selecting appropriate benchmark sites (as relatively intact ecosystems to use as reference sites), and identifying diverse locally appropriate native species suitable for each site. A restoration approach based on these can be selected, deployed, and subjected to continuous or regular assessments and monitoring to aid in course corrections. What ecological restoration is certainly *not* is a mindless tree-planting exercise to re-establish green cover without consideration of the above aspects.

Natural regeneration may be a more meaningful strategy than more interventional approaches in many large forest landscapes,[16] especially where degraded sites are close to existing tracts of undisturbed forests.[17] This may be the best approach to use in formerly logged forests that abut contiguous tracts in the Andamans. In more highly degraded sites, sites with poor natural regeneration, or in isolated forest fragments, active or reconstructive restoration could be undertaken. This would require dedicated surveys to identify sites, efforts such as the removal of invasive alien plants, creation of native plant nurseries with high diversity of native plant species characteristic of the islands' forests, and subsequent site preparation, planting and multi-year maintenance. In most cases where meaningful ecological restoration like this has been achieved in other parts of the world, it has been in the range of few hectares to tens of hectares, rather than over thousands of hectares as envisaged in the Lysenkoist plans behind the mega infrastructure project.

Even with such intensive efforts, only partial recovery can be achieved in complex ecosystems such as rainforests that have a large diversity of interacting species. Experiences from rainforest restoration in the Western Ghats indicate that forest attributes such as canopy cover, above ground carbon storage, adult tree and sapling density and species density, and compositional similarity to relatively undisturbed benchmarks may increase by 14–82 per cent over a span of about fifteen years.[18] This suggests, as does research from other parts of the world, that tropical forest ecosystems may take over hundred years to recover to levels approaching those in undamaged forests, while some attributes including the return of rare and endemic species may take centuries[19] or be irrecoverably lost forever.

Coral Reef Restoration—Is It Ever a Meaningful Solution?

While there is a long history of terrestrial restoration, the restoration of marine ecosystems is much more recent. In the past two decades, in the wake of rapidly declining coastal habitats, efforts at restoring mangroves, seagrass meadows, coral reefs and algal forests have grown in scope and ambition. The results are decidedly mixed. This has not stopped agencies around the world from promoting marine restoration as the bright beacon of hope for marine conservation. Coral reef restoration efforts have burgeoned in recent times, with most using one of four broad approaches: relocation of adult coral, coral gardening in nurseries, the creation of artificial reefs or the stabilisation of loose substrate. Among the more experimental approaches being explored are micro-fragmenting of massive corals that can then be used to 're-skin' dead colonies, and the creation of genetically modified super-coral to resist bleaching. Salvage operations such as the one the ZSI proposes represent a fifth of all recorded restoration projects.

So, are they effective? Well, a lot depends on what you mean by effectiveness. Most coral restoration projects measure their effectiveness by tracking the survivorship of coral—either young nursery transplants or translocated adults. According to published literature,[20] coral survival in restored areas can be as high as 70 per cent although the ZSI reports a 90 per cent survival rate for its own earlier projects.[21] What is important to remember, however, is that most restoration projects for which we have reliable information have been monitored for less than two years, and measures of longer-term survivorship are much more difficult to come by. More often than not, after several years of successful restoration, restored corals die en masse when a major storm comes through or when an ocean warming event causes mass bleaching of coral. The majority of restoration projects use fast-growing branching species; while they are able to occupy reef areas quickly, they are also among the most vulnerable to disturbance.

Highlights

- If the forests are destroyed for the project on Great Nicobar, their loss will be complete, irreversible and irreplaceable.
- Regarding the plans for coral reef restoration, it must be underlined that translocating reefs does not constitute the restoration of the reef as a living ecosystem. It does not guarantee the integrity and health of the reef.
- Besides, it is doubtful whether any amount of restoration would be meaningful in the face of increasing heat stress in a bleaching hot spot like the Nicobar waters.

A more pertinent question is how ecologically meaningful most coral restoration efforts are. A recent review of restoration projects across the tropics shows that most of them are positively tiny (a median size of 71 square metres, or about one-twentieth the size of an Olympic swimming pool) compared with the size of most reefs. Restoration efforts at more ecologically meaningful spatial and temporal scales are rare: less than 4 per cent of recorded projects have attempted anything more than a hectare, according to a recent review by Hughes and others.[22] There is a good reason projects are not larger: the costs and effort involved in genuinely scaling up restoration to ecologically meaningful sizes can be prohibitive. These costs can range from $50,000 to a whopping $1 million a hectare of reef restored (Rs 41 lakh to Rs 8.3 crore a hectare).

There are even more critical questions worth posing. Evaluating the effectiveness of a restoration project by focusing on the survivorship of coral is to conflate an indicator with a target. Yes, the fact that transplanted coral survive is an inherently good thing. But that is rather a far cry from restoring a healthy reef. Corals are among the most important architectural elements of a reef, but a reef is more than coral. The reef is a vibrant assemblage of dynamic and diverse relationships, full of complex flows of material and energy, held together with myriad interactions and behaviours that together form a suite of essential functions that determine how healthy the ecosystem is. And while it may be possible on living reefs to capture much of this complexity in simple measures of coral cover and survival, for restoration projects to use this as their primary measure of success is to misunderstand what the index was meant to stand in for in the first place. To say it more bluntly: a barge-full of transplanted coral does not constitute a reef, just as a vacant lot packed with prefabricated houses is not, by any stretch of the imagination, a bustling metropolis.

Perhaps the most important question in evaluating the effectiveness of coral restoration is what problem it is meant to solve. To hear its enthusiastic proponents, restoration is the conservation action of the future—necessary to reverse the spate of bad news we constantly hear from tropical reefs. As climate change and habitat destruction destroy vast swathes of reef area, our best hope for reefs is to invest in large-scale restoration of degraded patches. And if we can use these same techniques to facilitate large-scale developmental projects by shifting an inconvenient ecosystem to a place where it will not be a bother, why not?

Yet, if past results are anything to go by, it is clear that these claims are either wildly optimistic or cynically disingenuous. Getting coral to grow or translocating it, no matter how forcibly we do it, does not constitute the restoration of the reef as a living ecosystem. It does not guarantee that the integrity and health of the reef are preserved in all its dynamic bounty. Nor is it a solution to the problems of climate change. It cannot, even at its most effective, address the ecosystem-scale challenges that modern reefs face. As a recent commentary in *Nature Climate Change* insisted,[23] coral restoration is at best a feel-good palliative action that has little to do with saving coral reefs. If we are serious about conserving reefs, the authors claim, we do not need heroic interventions but more studied, transformative and systemic solutions based on what is known about how these complex social-ecological systems work. We need urgent action on climate change. And we need to ask hard questions about what we, as a society, would like to privilege when managing coral reefs and the human communities dependent on them.

What would those transformative solutions look like at the local level? For one, they would start with addressing the problems at their source rather than seeking Band-Aid remedies at the point of impact. More often than not, ecosystems have a remarkable ability to recover their inherent functions once pressures reduce, and the best hope of restoration is to support this inherent capacity. For another, it is critical to recognise the primacy of place. It is a corruption of the restoration project to believe that ecosystems are formed of Lysenkoist species, endlessly protean, able to be engineered into any chimeric form the state decides, transplanted to flourish in more convenient locations, outside the steamrollers of progress.

An ecosystem is more than a ragbag of species, thrown together by chance and circumstance. Species interact, with each other and with the environment around them. In the dialectical relationship between species and habitats, ecosystems are created, maintained and transformed. If restoration is to rescue itself from being merely a convenient instrument of a developmentalist state, it needs to focus not so much on the survival of individuals as on the restoration of broken relationships between species and habitats, and on the supporting of critical functions and processes that hold ecosystems together. This is clearly a harder task than compensatory afforestation or translocating colonies with chainsaws and epoxy, and will need more careful understanding of how these ecosystems work, their resilience against all the forces of change and their ultimate vulnerabilities.

So what then should we make of the Galathea Bay recommendations? While the project plans appear to be primarily economy and tourism oriented, reports have suggested a strategic relevance as well of Great Nicobar for the Indian government. A project oriented towards defence or strategic purposes would, however, likely require much less area and cause less damage than the transshipment port, airport, greenfield township and tourism. Regardless of the scale of the operation, we have to acknowledge that the attempt at compensatory afforestation will certainly not suffice to replace the lost rainforests of Great Nicobar even if tree planting is carried out over ten times the area in the completely different ecosystems of the Aravallis or central India. Restorative efforts often focus on measures such as area covered, number of saplings planted, or at best plant survival in the near-term (two to three years).

None of these indicators is a sufficient measure of the recovery of an ecosystem dominated by long-lived organisms like trees that may live for 300–500 years or more. While there is a limited role for ecological restoration in rainforests that were formerly reduced to a highly degraded state, nothing in contemporary research suggests that destroying intact old-growth tropical rainforests such as those on Great Nicobar can ever be sufficiently recovered or compensated for by such measures as are known today.

Similarly, can reef-salvaging operations of the kind being proposed for the region ever be justified? Even if we were to ignore the logistic challenges and expenses involved, we would still be left with the vexing question of what exactly we would achieve by translocating 16,000 coral individuals from one bay to another. A recent study of bleaching susceptibility during the 2016 El Niño event[24] showed that the Nicobar region was particularly susceptible to high sea surface temperatures. As we write this, the retreating El Niño of 2023-24 has left dramatic scars on reefs across the world, and although no independent researchers can survey the Nicobar reefs, sea surface temperatures have been soaring, with bleaching warnings unusually persistent in Great Nicobar waters.

This raises difficult questions about how meaningful any amount of restoration would be in the face of increasing heat stress in a bleaching hotspot. It is difficult to know how many of the 8,900 Acropora individuals (apart from the rest) have survived the current El Niño, and whether they will survive the next heatwave when it hits in the next few years. Even if they do, what do we gain with their translocation? At best, we would have committed a grand violence on a living ecosystem to create a caricature version of one, which we would then dress up as an ecological rescue operation, held together with epoxy.

What Are the Options?

What then are the options before us? One that deserves serious consideration is to send the project back to the drawing board to avoid the large-scale transformation that a city, port and tourism will cause. A reconsideration of the project focused on strengthening strategic needs while safeguarding existing forests and Shompen territories and addressing the needs of the great Nicobarese, including their return to their ancestral lands, would be very worthwhile. The more limited impact on Great Nicobar ecosystems could then be addressed with a critical conversation about ecological restoration in all its flavours. We can make careful accounting of when it works and under what sets of circumstances. This conversation needs to focus on the techniques we use, how ecologically and socially meaningful the outcomes are, the metrics we use to evaluate these outcomes, and the costs of these interventions. We can undertake a critical, deep, cross-sectoral reckoning about why we need to use these approaches in the first place, and what it is we are giving up when we resort to them. Above all, like every potentially beautiful solution, we need to be mindful of when it is a legitimate response to the problem at hand and when it is merely a lazy and cynical sleight of hand dressed up as a panacea.

But how can we view the restoration plans if the development is a fait accompli, as it appears to be at present? Then, it becomes our duty as a scientific community not to validate a planned ecological catastrophe with palliative fixes. It makes us complicit in a double ecological duplicity. The first is subterfuge that the impacts of the development are unlikely to be large in the first place. The second, and perhaps more pernicious, is that it perpetuates the notion that there is no engineering violence we can impose on the world that cannot be solved with just a little more engineering. The truth is that ecological systems and the functions they embody cannot be engineered in and out of existence without considering their uniqueness of geography, their peculiarities of environment and the contingencies of history.

A more honest response then? Declare the ecosystem dead. Declare it dead in large cautionary letters. Document its passing in numbers and in words. Enumerate not merely the trees and corals that were lost but the countless other species, present and future, for whom the ecosystem will no longer be home. In its obituary, list down all the functions and services the ecosystem provided. Speak as eloquently as we can of the rich unwritten history that has been erased. Sit quietly with the loss, along with the peoples for whom this loss means more than it would ever mean for us. Mourn this loss with civility. Bear witness to the fact that these ecosystems, unknowable in their complexity, made way for a certain idea of material progress, a vision of modernity, and a signal to the world about who we are as a nation and what we are capable of.

The reckoning will come later. As with Lysenkoism, it may come much, much later. And when it does, our bearing of witness will have served its purpose. Does this serve as restorative justice? Perhaps not. But, as a community that cares deeply about the ecosystems that sustain us, this is the truest thing we can do.

(First published in *Frontline*, 3 March 2025.)

12

A Threat to Wildlife

Saurav Harikumar

The islands are home to a rare mix of wildlife found nowhere else on Earth. Here are ten that face the greatest threat from the Great Nicobar project.

Having been isolated for a long time on an ecological timescale, the Nicobar Islands are fertile ground for speciation, or the evolution of new species. The islands thus form a unique ecological niche, with a great proportion of the species at risk of extinction. The following creatures are some of those endangered by the Great Nicobar project:

1) The Nicobar megapode (*Megapodius nicobariensis*)

The Nicobar megapode, which has been listed as 'vulnerable to extinction' under the International Union for Conservation of Nature (IUCN) Red List, is found only in Nicobar. Named for their enormous feet (mega–large; poda–foot) that resemble those of prehistoric species, these pheasant-like birds are becoming an increasingly rare sight in the islands they call home.

A deep dive into megapode behaviour reveals why this animal is commonly known as the 'thermometer bird'. Megapodes characteristically lay their eggs in nests of sand, mud and organic debris built into mounds. Their active nesting mounds can be as large as 10 cubic metres, which is remarkable as the birds grow only to a fraction of the size of their nests. Microbial activity in the organic matter within the nests, which is the primary source of heat for the incubation of the eggs, maintains the heat constantly at 33 degrees Celsius. Young chicks hatch fully feathered with the ability to immediately fly, minimising any parental investment.

Today, the population of the Nicobar megapode is restricted to only two islands, Great Nicobar being one of them. The bay where the Galathea River empties into the Andaman Sea (also the Galathea Bay Wildlife Sanctuary) is a hotspot with seven active nesting mounds that are likely to be destroyed by the government's megaproject. The environmental clearance granted to the project, island-wide, has declared that thirty of the fifty-one mounds are situated in the project site and will be permanently destroyed.

A behavioural flight response in most avians, including megapodes which are extremely shy and sensitive creatures, is to completely abandon their nests in the face of danger or unfamiliar stimuli in the environment. Considering how rare breeding pairs are, the infrequent mating events and the fact that eggs take two to three months to hatch, one can only imagine how devastating the new disturbance-filled environment of a shipping terminal will be on these remarkable architect species.

2) Nicobar treeshrew (*Tupaia nicobarica*)

The Nicobar treeshrew goes largely unnoticed, spending its time high in the canopies for most of its life. Although they have the suffix -shrew in their names, they in fact form their own mammalian order, and are more closely related to primates than squirrels or true shrews. The treeshrew in Nicobar is brown-orange all along its elongated face and bushy tail, while adult torsos tend to have darker greyish fur.

The diurnal animal is an insectivore-frugivore that plays a vital role in the management of pest-insect species as well as seed dispersal of those fruits whose seeds they do not consume. The treeshrew is vital to the food chain as it is an important prey of many snake and bird species on the island.

It is one of only four native mammalian species on the terrestrial portion of the island (the others being the wild boar, long-tailed macaques and a number of chiropterans) and thereby creates a rather unique ecological niche that no other species can fill. Some studies theorise that treeshrews might be monogamous, that is, they will only form a single breeding pair in their lives. They are also intelligent animals that have been known to form long-lasting feeding relationships with birds like the racket-tailed drongos.

Treeshrews are shy and notably avoid humans. Notoriously difficult to find and photograph, these creatures are almost entirely absent in urban and suburban zones and prefer secluded interior forest systems like the Great Nicobar Biodiversity Reserve or Galathea National Park. The IUCN Red List currently labels them as endangered.

3) Great Nicobar serpent eagle (*Spilornis klossi*)

Only in the past five years has the Great Nicobar serpent eagle been considered its own species. They had formerly been considered a subspecies of a much wider ranging species—the crested serpent eagle (*Spilornis cheela*) which also inhabit these islands. The accipiter (the genus of birds of prey) diversity is remarkable in these islands, with about fifteen to eighteen different species of harrier, sparrowhawk, kite, buzzard, baza and eagle all co-inhabiting this system. Yet, the Great Nicobar serpent eagle is especially uncommon and unique.

By some accounts, this bird is the smallest known species of eagle on the planet. Going by their name, snakes account for a solid portion of the serpent eagle's prey. However, it has a broader diet that includes other reptiles, frogs, birds and small mammals. Like the crested serpent eagle, these birds also have a bunch of darker feathers on their head that forms a crest-like tuft. They have a short tail and two powerful talons.

As the Great Nicobar serpent eagle is a new bird species, there are significant knowledge gaps about its behaviour, habitat preferences or tolerance to humans, but what we do know is that it is endemic to the Great Nicobar Island and listed as endangered on the IUCN Red List. While some accipiters like kites are prime examples of generalist, human-tolerant species, serpent eagles do not share that mindset. They are very rarely sighted alongside settlements or towns and prefer rural farmland or undisturbed forest systems.

4) Nicobari pig (*Sus scrofa nicobaricus*)

Wild boar in general are a widespread group of mammals, and often are so successful in colonising new landscapes that they have become invasive in many parts of the world. However, these opportunistic, generalist species, like so many other fauna in these isolated islands, underwent speciation on Great Nicobar sometime in our distant past, and the result was a subspecies known as the Nicobari pig.

Far more uncommon than their counterparts in similar systems like Indonesia or mainland India, the Nicobari pigs are restricted to reclusive, semi-feral populations. They have dark fur and a sturdy short frame. A mane running from the head to the lower back is a defining feature.

Evidence suggests they have been outcompeted by the domestic pig, goat or sheep variants; or been hunted by feral dog populations—both of which are invasive species introduced to Great Nicobar. Since there are no other ungulates (large mammals with hooves) on the island like deer, the pig is the biggest wild mammal on the island and thus occupies a niche no other species can replace. It forms a vital prey base for apex predators like crocodiles and is extremely important to the indigenous Shompen and Nicobarese tribes who rely upon it as a primary source of meat. The Nicobarese share a close, special relationship with the wild pig, and regard it as the 'food of their ancestors'.

5) Nicobar scops owl (*Otus alius*)

The Nicobar scops owl is a large endemic owl species defined by brilliant yellow eyes set on a brown head and body defined by streaks of grey or white plumage, particularly around the head and breast. It is nocturnal and an adept hunter, scouring the forest floor for insects and arachnids, lizards or frogs.

A common story with highly endemic, understudied island species—very little is known of this bird's ecology. Like most owls, their bodies are adapted to flying in silence, and their low melancholic vocalisations rising in scale are often the only indication of their presence. They have been spotted in a wide range of habitat types, from the eastern coast all the way to the interior forests of the Great Nicobar Biosphere Reserve.

Until recently, there wasn't enough data on this bird to identify how threatened it is. While there still has been no population survey, according to existing literature, there are just over a thousand mature individuals are left on Great Nicobar, which constitutes their largest population. This has earned it a 'near threatened' label on the IUCN Red List, and population numbers are predicted to decline due to habitat loss as well as anthropogenic hunting/snaring or the use of illegal pesticides.

6) Daniel's forest lizard (*Bronchocela danieli*)

Nicobar is a haven for reptile enthusiasts, with its hyper-diverse group of species ranging from skinks and geckos to turtles, monitors and even crocodilians. One species on many checklists is the Daniel's forest lizard, also known as Daniel's bloodsucker.

This lizard, a bright green splash of colour with a yellow and black patch just behind the eyes, is semi-arboreal and spends much of its time on low trees and bushes. It is characterised by an impossibly long tail, often comfortably twice the size of its body. Like most bloodsucker lizards, it can change its colour to match its surroundings. It preys on moths, butterflies, dragonflies and flies. Like other species of its genus, it is oviparous and lays its eggs in loose earth or sand.

All current observations of this lizard have placed this species as endemic to the surroundings of Campbell Bay in Great Nicobar. It is currently classified by IUCN under 'least concern'. However, research on its true population density or range has never been carried out.

7) Saltwater crocodile (*Crocodylus porosus*)

The largest living reptile on the planet, the saltwater crocodile occupies its well-deserved position as the apex predator on these islands. Growing up to 6 metres and reaching weights of 1,000–

1,500 kilograms, these relics of prehistoric times are some of the most imposing animals to exist.

Bright yellow with black markings when young and dark greenish grey when adults, these are ambush predators, despite their bulk. Their prey range from sharks, fresh or saltwater fish, and other reptiles to crustaceans, birds and mammals. They are the only species on the island that the local government has issued warnings about with signposts on beaches or creeks. There is no end to the amount of scientific literature highlighting the status of an apex predator in an ecological system, and the role the crocodile plays in Great Nicobar makes it irreplaceable.

A report submitted by the Wildlife Institute of India in July 2022 for the conservation and management of the saltwater crocodile states that of the 195 kilometres of coastline of the island, 77 kilometres of crocodile habitat is likely to be affected by the shipping project's activities. The proposed airport is to be set up on a wetland which is going to be designated as a 'crocodile-free zone', and any crocodile found there is to be translocated and radio tagged/satellite tagged before it is released in the wild. While a crocodile rescue and rehabilitation centre is proposed, it will only be able to support a maximum of fifty captive individuals.

Looking out over the inappropriately named 'Mugger' Nala, one can spot the 'salties' lounging barely a few kilometres from Campbell Bay. Reports of farmers encountering them in plantations inundated by water post the 2004 tsunami stand testament to this species' resilience and ability to adapt. However, no amount of generalism can compensate for the widespread habitat loss or the disturbance they are going to be subjected to, and the new megaproject might very well kickstart the salties' slow crawl towards local extinction.

8) Nicobar cat snake (*Boiga wallachi*)

A strange phenomenon observed in Great Nicobar is the striking absence of venomous snakes such as cobras, vipers, and kraits (except the sea krait). This is unusual since northern and central Nicobar have over five unique species of endemic pit vipers and Indonesia to the south-east is overflowing with venomous species. The closest thing Great Nicobar has to a mildly venomous species is the Nicobar cat snake, an endemic species found nowhere else on the planet.

An olive-coloured snake, with dark rounded blotches, the Nicobar cat snake is almost fully terrestrial and nocturnal, hunting rodents and frogs. Birds' eggs also form part of its diet. The snakes are characterised by long bodies with large heads and big cat-like eyes, which gives them their genus name.

IUCN has rated this species as 'data deficient', as there have never been any surveys to estimate its density or abundance. There is no protection currently for the species, and locals sometimes encounter this animal in coops as it hunts for domestic chicken eggs. Widespread habitat loss is pushing this species towards settlements where conflict with humans is leading to further harm.

9) Omura's whale (*Balaenoptera omurai*)

As little as we know about the species inhabiting the rainforests on the island, we know even less about the oceans surrounding it. The oceans teem with life often unexplored, undocumented and likely at risk of going extinct before they have even been discovered.

Nicobar's coastline sports numerous coral reefs teeming with marine life. From tiny anemones all the way to the biggest creatures on the planet, this spectrum of diversity even puts the rainforests above ground to shame.

The Omura's whale is a species inhabiting the Indo-Pacific ocean system and has been sighted a few times off the coast of the Andaman and Nicobar Islands. It is one of the smallest of the rorqual whales (a type of whale with pleated skin) and was identified as a distinct species only in 2003. Very little is known of its ecology or habitat preferences. They are filter feeders, whose main diet is believed to be the almost planktonic-sized krill.

The Environment Impact Assessment (EIA) report for the development plan does not even acknowledge this species and twelve other cetacean species (species that include whales, porpoises and dolphins) that inhabit the waters around these islands. While not sedentary organisms, all these species, Omura's whale included, are terribly impacted by habitat loss globally. In fact, even their presence in these waters is a wonderous thing. They are classified under the 'data deficient' category on the IUCN Red List, and their populations are steadily declining. Whales are terribly sensitive to sound and there is enough scientific data to show that shipping impacts their abundance.

10) False killer whale (*Pseudorca crassidens*)

Even though it sports 'whale' in its name, this is a species of dolphin. The only extant member of the Pseudorca genus, the false killer whale is named thus because its skull structure is similar to that of the orca. A species found on almost every single coastline in the world, this is a highly social animal that forms pods of up to fifty animals.

Black or grey on top and lighter on the underside, they can reach a weight of 2,300 kilograms and grow up to 20 feet in length. A remarkably intelligent species, the whales form everlasting bonds with members of their own pods, and also with members of other species like dolphins. They have been observed responding to distress calls from other species against predators like sharks. They have even been reported interacting sexually with bottlenose dolphins in the wild. False killer whales use echolocation to navigate and find prey. They are viviparous and give birth to their young, like all mammals.

Classified as 'near threatened' on the IUCN Red List, the false killer whale is another species whose presence in the Nicobar waters could soon be a thing of the past, if the Union government goes ahead with its proposed plans.

(First published as 'On the brink: 10 endangered species of the Nicobar Islands', in *Frontline*, 3 March 2025.)

12a

First Animal: Poems and Drawings

Tansy Troy

Daniel's Forest Lizard

Bright green
whip of colour
I, Daniel's Forest Lizard
do not deserve to be ousted
or outcast.

Leatherback Turtle

On my leather back shell
the universe once rested.

Now, I as dive deep, think:
in this moment, do you want to
swim,
drown
or sink?

Nicobar Cat Snake

There's no sting in my tail,
no wrath in my venom:
the only poison is the
catastrophic plan to destroy
my Cat Snake home.

Omura's Whale

Shipping
impacts my
sensitive sonar:
I, King Omura,
whale of turquoise soma.

A Triptych for the Nicobar Megapode

Big foot
with bigger heart
shyly I scratch sand-mud-grass nest,
laying vast ancestral eggs-chicks who

fly up
without needing
my tutelage
full-feathered, utterly evolved—
wise young birds:

Left in the peace I deeply cherish.
I, architect of crone earth,
could build us all a future.

Nicobar Serpent Eagle

Tiniest accipiter,
my reclusive mindset deserves
utmost respect.

Nicobar Scops Owl

Shining out of the darkened forest,
golden-eyed jewel.

Spell of the Saltwater Crocodile

Snap snap!
Crocodylus eats all madness,
swallows whole all Sambelong,
never letting go.

This homeland of the Shompen
my prehistoric armour defends.

Though you may enjoy the gift of candid speech,
yet I must teach you the power of Spell.

Slap slap!
tail on mudslime
supple-spined, I journey on
to other worlds.

Nicobar Treeshrew

I am a Treeshrew
who must speak to you—
must discuss and long debate
the treachery of this isle.

My highly elongated brow
and shrewd distain for camera traps,
does not preclude my all-night networking
with racket-tailed drongos.

I invite you to our wild AGM.
Venue: clouds of leaf, of bark.
Our pressing agenda: your sweet survival.
Attend.
Dates TBC.

Pseudorca Crassidens: a plea to be true to the False Killer Whale

I am
not false,
just an orca-like dolphin whale
on the Red List: my once sacred presence
now deemed
History

unless
you commit to my
mammalian offspring,
forge fast family bonds,
perhaps we will never know
truth of the word tribe.

EXPERT SPEAK

13

Questioning Government Claims

RISHIKA PARDIKAR

The Union government is currently pushing through a Rs 72,000 crore megaproject in the Great Nicobar Island without the consent, or taking into account the concerns of, the Nicobarese and the Shompen—the tribes that have inhabited the islands for thousands of years. This is what a senior former government official from the Andaman and Nicobar Islands had to say about the Great Nicobar project.

On 28 August 2024, the Andaman and Nicobar Islands Integrated Development Corporation (ANIIDCO), the main implementing agency, called for proposals by 30 September to begin cutting about a million trees for the project, which includes a container port, an international airport, a town, roads and tourism resorts.

The government of Prime Minister Narendra Modi has not conducted any meaningful discussion with the Nicobarese about the project and has had no discussions with the Shompen, who communicate in a unique language that is yet to be deciphered.

In an interview, Anstice Justin, seventy, former Deputy Director, Anthropological Survey of India (AnSI) and a Nicobarese, spoke at length about the tribal communities to whom the island is home and the threats posed to them by the mega infrastructure project.

Justin's native name is Asenga Ta-aunj. He was born in Car Nicobar, one of the twenty-two Nicobarese islands, of which twelve are inhabited, and lives in Port Blair, the capital of the Andaman and Nicobar Islands, renamed Sri Vijaya Puram on 13 September 2024.

On 21 August, the Union Minister of Environment, Forest and Climate Change, Bhupender Yadav, responding to a letter from Jairam Ramesh (see Annexure 2), Congress member of parliament and former Union Minister of Environment and Forests, claimed 'legal safeguards and constitutional provisions related to the tribal communities have been duly followed'.

This is not true.

Justin agreed with Ramesh's warning about 'the grave threat' that the project posed to the island's tribal communities and its rainforests and challenged Yadav's claims.

'Has the environment minister conducted an assessment? Has he ever talked to the Shompen or the Nicobarese about the problems they are facing and the other ground realities?' said Justin. 'We do not understand the language of the Shompen but this is not the only problem. We are imposing "development" on them.'

In September 2023, *Article 14* reported how the megaproject intends to take over the ancestral lands of the Nicobarese, where they lived before the 2004 tsunami, by listing them as 'uninhabited'. In November 2022, as we reported, the Nicobarese tribal council withdrew consent for the 'diversion' of forests, an official term that refers to clearance to cut them down. The chairman of the local tribal council said the government had rushed them to initially agree without giving them enough information or time for consultations.

Ramesh, too, pointed to these issues in another letter he wrote to Bhupender Yadav on 27 August. He referred to safeguards under the Shompen Policy framed in 2015, which recognises the 'integrity' of the community. This integrity, Ramesh said, is threatened by the project. The project would require 'permanent displacement' of the Nicobarese from their ancestral villages, he added.

On 29 September, Ramesh again wrote to Yadav, accusing the government of inviting proposals to begin cutting Great Nicobar's forests even as the National Green Tribunal hears petitions against the project. 'I believe the government of India is hell-bent on inflicting an ecological and humanitarian disaster on our country,' wrote Ramesh. The forests to be cut are supposed to be replaced by 'compensatory afforestation' in Haryana.

In April 2023, the National Commission for Scheduled Tribes (NCST) also raised concerns about the violation of forest rights of local communities. The NCST is a constitutional body meant to safeguard rights of tribal communities and investigate violations.

Justin's primary and secondary education were in Car Nicobar, after which he moved to Port Blair for higher education and then to the mainland to the Anthropology department at Ranchi University. He cleared the Union Public Service Commission (UPSC) examinations for civil services and joined the regional centre of AnSI in Port Blair. Excerpts from the interview with Anstice Justin:

Q. Recently, the Union environment minister Bhupender Yadav and former environment minister Jairam Ramesh discussed the Great Nicobar project in a series of letters. Ramesh pointed to ecological and tribal rights concerns. In response,

Yadav claimed, among other things, that legal safeguards and constitutional provisions related to tribal communities had been followed. What do you make of his exchange?

We have read the statements made by the environment minister and the response from Jairam Ramesh. Shompen and Nicobarese villages like Chingen and Kokeon will be affected by the project. But has the environment minister conducted an assessment? Has he talked to the Shompen? The Shompen are least concerned with the administration and they are misunderstood by ministers and policymakers. This is not safeguarding [tribal rights] in the real sense. Has the minister ever talked to the Shompen or the Nicobarese about the problems they are facing and the other ground realities? We do not understand the language of the Shompen but this is not the only problem. We are imposing 'development' on them.

Q. What do you think about the mega project? How do you think it would affect the Nicobarese and the Shompen and the local ecology?

Let us understand the forest and the people who are native to these forests. The Shompen are a particularly vulnerable tribal group. They are semi-nomads. And then there are the Nicobarese who are more 'contemporary'.

'Shompen' is what the Nicobarese call them. It is a distorted form of 'Shamhanp' or 'Somhanp', which means forest dweller. In earlier literature, it was spelt 'Shom Pen'. Till today, we do not know how the Shompen identify themselves. They prefer a life of their own. Sometimes, some of them come out of the forest to gather fishing lines and hook from the Andaman Adim Janjati Vikas Samiti (AAJVS) and also the Nicobarese with whom they share a reciprocal bartering system. During this time, AAJVS offers them ration which they gladly accept.[1] But this does not mean they are dependent on AAJVS or that they come to Campbell Bay to collect ration.

The Shompen are usually not concerned about the Andaman and Nicobar administration. They practise animism, which is nature worship. The project will destroy nature. We will be destroying their source of sustenance and foraging grounds. To them, nature is sacred and similar to temples, churches and mosques. Do we destroy our places of worship? When we have no respect for the beliefs of people, our approach to develop the area is very profane and unconsecrated.

The Shompen believe in a nature–man–spirit relationship. It is man-to-man cultural ecology, which they employ for practical purposes like collective hunting-gathering activities, raising edible roots, construction of their traditional dwellings, etc. They have immense knowledge of forests, other terrestrial resources and also aquatic bodies, creeks, morass lands, swamps, the sea ... there is a totality of the sacredness of nature which we cannot isolate from the survival of the Shompen.

Many times, I have learnt a lot from the Shompen. Once they led us into the interior forests, and we were not allowed to cut leaves of small trees, stems of trees, weeds or even bushes to mark the pathway that could assist in returning to the main metalled road. So, we were astray for some time. But just imagine and contemplate this kind of respect to the tiniest, obnoxious weeds, trees, leaves, because they believe there is life in them all.

Now coming to the Nicobarese, they practise Christianity but it is not like the Christianity we see in European countries. It is Christianity blended with syncretic elements because they also have their own beliefs. It is a peaceful coexistence of Christianity with animism.

After the tsunami in 2004, many Nicobarese were displaced and they have been living in tsunami shelters which the government has turned into permanent shelters. But they have not been given land for cultivation. The project is coming up on ancestral land of the Nicobarese where they lived before the tsunami.

There is a sense of betrayal among the Nicobarese community because their signatures for diversion of forest land for the project were taken by force and without providing correct information. They were made to attend the meeting without knowing the agenda. So, they withdrew their consent. With the Shompen, there is no dialogue at all! The government has not engaged in any dialogue with the Shompen about the mega project.

If there is a forest, we need to take care of the people who live in the forest. But this project is being imposed on the original inhabitants of the island without their consent.

Q. What kind of development do you need in the Nicobar islands? Before the 2024 general elections, I spoke to members of the Nicobarese community from Great Nicobar and also other islands, such as Nancowry and Car Nicobar. They spoke about the lack of good education facilities, limited ship connectivity to Port Blair, the need for roads and water supply and medical care. So, the Union government's view of development, basically limited to a mega port and an international airport, is very different from the kind of development the Nicobarese community seeks.

This is very true. There is no improvement in health facilities at primary health centres (PHCs) in Great Nicobar. PHCs only have general medical officers and nurses. There are no specialists. For many pregnancy-related issues, women are referred to hospitals in Port Blair. There was a recent case where, after a dialysis unit was opened, we found out that there was no technician. So, the purpose of installing the dialysis unit is defeated.

We also face issues of shortage of medicines and sometimes, hospitals do not get tap water supply. Water is the elixir of life but in the Nicobar Islands, this is the reality we face. And of course, the quality of education in government schools ... Everyone can understand what it is. Connectivity to Port Blair is another issue. Sailing schedules of ships are erratic. [Flight] services are available Monday and Saturday, but priority is given for defence personnel. The condition of our roads is also very bad with potholes and stagnated water. The quality of internet facilities is excruciatingly painful for aspiring young people. Come and reside in the remotest villages in Great Nicobar and you will see the kind of situations we are coping with.

I studied in a vernacular school [where the medium of instruction is a mix of Nicobarese and English] in Car Nicobar. There were no trained teachers. Currently, the education system is somewhat better than those days but it is still not very good.

To my mind, policymakers and administrators have not taken care of these issues. Without looking at ground realities like hospitals and schools, how can we have development? There is a lot of talk about tourism but not about upgrading health facilities at PHCs. A country should be able to provide good health facilities to her citizens.

Q. Is employment also an issue in Nicobar islands? Do people prefer to migrate to Port Blair or to the mainland for jobs?

You see, employment opportunities in Car Nicobar and Great Nicobar are the same as seen elsewhere in the country

Q. Do you believe there are parallels between how the development of the Andaman Trunk Road impacted the Jarawas (a tribe) and how this mega project could impact the Nicobarese

and the Shompen? Are there any lessons to be learnt from past mistakes?

This is an issue which is very close to my heart. I had discussed it in many meetings with the Ministry of Tribal Affairs during my service.

With the Jarawas, the official government policy is 'maximum autonomy with minimum intervention'. But as you know, rules and policies can be violated. And of course, there are lessons to be learnt. The situation with the interactions between the settlers and the Jarawa is deplorable. There were reports of molestation of Jarawa women and encroachment of forests. The road disturbed their foraging and hunting grounds and they were made welfare-dependent people.[2]

Q. The Tribal Council of Great Nicobar and Little Nicobar has written multiple letters on a variety of issues, such as the opposition to the declaration of wildlife sanctuaries in the islands to compensate for the loss of biodiversity from the megaproject and the withdrawal of their consent for diversion of forest land. But they have never received a response, neither from the Union government nor from the Andaman and Nicobar administration. What do you make of this?

The original inhabitants of the island are a miniscule population. All I can say is the Nicobarese have tried their best to protest against the megaproject. But none of the policymakers are reading the representations they sent time after time. The Nicobarese feel cheated. We can only lament about this.

There were some incidents in the past when we were near Shompen settlements and they made gestures which, to me, seemed like they were saying do not intrude on our lands. These were codable gestures. They were reluctant to meet us.

Q. We do not understand the language of the Shompen. In this context, do you believe it is possible to obtain informed consent of the Shompen for the megaproject?

We need genuine consent and approval from the native populations. Development can take place only after this. Now here is a situation where a language barrier exists. How can we tell them about this megaproject? Even AAJVS officials cannot communicate with the Shompen. With the help of interpreters, we can touch some overt aspects of their culture. But what about covert aspects?

The Shompen are not concerned about the overtures of the administration, leave alone development. They live a life of their own.

Can we barricade the Shompen? Turn the forests into a zoo? The Shompen may have their own grievances. But who will understand their anxieties?

(First published as 'Nicobarese anthropologist and former officer questions Modi govt claims over controversial Great Nicobar project', in *Article 14*, 30 September 2024.)

14

A Can of Worms

Vaishnavi Rathore

One of the questions raised by former environment minister Jairam Ramesh in his correspondence with current minister Bhupender Yadav about the Great Nicobar Project (Annexure 2) refers to a video report prepared by anthropologist Vishvajit Pandya.

The report 'shows members of the Shompen community clearly stating that they are against any disturbances to their forested and riparian habitats', Ramesh's letter notes.

A largely uncontacted tribe of about 250 people, the Shompens live on the Great Nicobar Island, the southernmost landmass of India. In 2021, the Modi government announced plans to develop a massive infrastructural project on the island at a cost of Rs 72,000 crore, which many fear could endanger the island's native tribal communities and unique flora and fauna.

In the run-up to the announcement, the administration of the Andaman and Nicobar Islands formed an empowered committee to examine proposals drafted by the government think-tank NITI Aayog for the 'development of various projects' on the Great Nicobar Island.

Among those on the committee was Dr Vishvajit Pandya, Professor of Anthropology at the Dhirubhai Ambani Institute of Information Communication Technology, Gujarat, who is also Founder and Honorary Director of the government-run Andaman and Nicobar Tribal Research and Training Institute.

Pandya submitted a video report to the administration, which included interviews he had conducted with members of the island's tribal communities, the Shompens and the Nicobarese, as well as settlers from the mainland who had been living there for decades. 'We never heard from the administration after that,' Pandya told *Scroll.in*.

In excerpts of the video report shown by Pandya at an online discussion, a Shompen man can be seen clearly stating: 'If you want to cut the forest, cut in on the coast. Do not climb our hills.'

The full report, however, was not made public by the administration nor was it included in the records of the empowered committee, according to the letter written by Ramesh. Pandya told *Scroll.in* that had the report been released, 'it would have been like opening a can of worms'.

Pandya first started ethnographic research in Little Andaman among the Onge tribal community in 1983 as a part of his doctoral work at the University of Chicago. Over the next three decades, the sixty-nine-year-old anthropologist was involved with both research and policy work related to islands' tribal communities, including the Jarawas and the Shompens. In 2015, he helped draft the administration's Shompen Policy.

Scroll.in spoke to him about the video report he prepared, and his views on the Great Nicobar Project. Excerpts from the interview:

Q. What was your team asked to do by the administration?

The administration was creating different small groups of people to go and give an assessment of the project. We were not told all the details of what the project was going to be. It was a very vague kind of thing that we want to develop Great Nicobar because it is a huge mass of land and somehow it has to be made into productive use. What that productive use was, was vaguely mentioned.

Q. What was the journey to meet the Shompen like?

I was going in as an anthropologist, and was expected to talk about the people in that environment, especially the Shompen. I decided that instead of me saying something, I should make the people's voices come to the desk of NITI Aayog and the administration in Port Blair. Instead of writing a report, [I thought] why don't I go there with a team of people and make a short film.

It was about a four-hour trek and then another four and a half hours for the return. We followed along the stream—that is a clearer way to walk, otherwise you would have to clear the forest, trample along the terrain. In some parts, you can cross with canoes if you are lucky enough to have those available. None of the Shompen live in a village where you can find them together. You would be lucky if you do.

Q. What were the broad points that you documented in the video report?

It is very easy to say that this project will impact the indigenous communities. But how will it impact them? That has remained unexplained. I wanted to find the reasoning from the Shompen themselves.

The Shompens have the argument that it will destroy the area's soil regeneration system. Each part of the forest is associated with streams of the Galathea and Alexandra rivers criss-crossing the island. When the river overflows in the rainy season, the alluvial soil is deposited downstream, which makes it possible for Shompens to regenerate their tapioca gardens and horticultural plots.

These plots are inherited through the matrilineal line amongst the Shompen. The girl's family gives those lands—it's like the sons go to work on their wife's lands. So, gardens and marriage are very important. The marriage is always held upstream, the girls come from the upstream and boys from the downstream. If the stream is blocked because of logging operations or building of the port, that could disrupt their kinship, marriage, and dependence on water and land. That's why they said in the video, 'You can stay in the coastal area, but don't come uphill in the forest.'

Land is not just a title of zameen. There is a social and cultural meaning of land. Sarkari babus will not understand this, and that's why we got the people to talk on camera.

The administration also showed us where they were planning to have the airport and gave us a vague idea of how they wanted to do ecotourism there, a place where people can come and enjoy natural features, habitats and forests, do some trekking, some type of a nature park, and wanted us to try to find a suitable location. So we talked to people and asked them what kind of development they would like there.

There is a Sikh community that is present in the Great Nicobar and when we interviewed them they said we were made to settle here, we have made this land cultivable, but where is the facility for our products to be marketed here? Even if someone falls sick there they depend on the helicopter to go to Port Blair. These were the more pertinent issues, they were not concerned about *kitne tourist aa rahe hai* (the potential tourist footfall).

Q. What were your expectations from the administration after you submitted the video report?

I was expecting that they would call for a much more in-depth explanation and study of the impacts. But, we never heard anything from the administration after that. Nothing—no thank you, no goodbye. The video was never released. No one wants to yield to [the recommendations] and it is of no consequence to the administration.

Q. Why do you think they never released the report?

Because it would be like opening a can of worms.

Q. What are the future aspirations of the Shompen?

See, there are other tribal groups on the Andaman and Nicobar Islands. And if you consider them on a spectrum, some of them want to have outside contact like the Great Andamanese. Some of them did not want it till recent times like Jarawas. Some like the Sentinelese—they have given a tough time to any outsiders.

Government reports used to call Shompens 'shy'. Hostile Jarawas, aggressive Sentinelese, docile Onges—these are the terms reports used. Why would the Shompen be shy? These are all the categories created because of the way [the administration] interacted with them and the way it suits the scheme of our development. Shompen are aware of the outside world and are articulate that they do not want the outsiders here. And that's why they became 'shy'.

Development for these tribes perhaps means good medical and other facilities that secures their life and improves its quality, and also ensures their dignity of existence, which has slowly been taken away from the groups on this spectrum.

For the Shompen, the government has said they will give them Aadhaar and make them vote. Have they explained to them what voting is, what the state is? No! They have no idea. This is like monkeys being made to dance in a circus.

Q. In your work at ANTRI (Andaman and Nicobar Tribal Research Institute), what were the kind of questions that came up for consideration?

We had said that first of all, there should not be one policy for all the tribes. They all have different kinds of economies and are at different stages of acculturation, and therefore one policy should not be applicable to all of them. There should be context sensitivity to policy formulation for each tribal community, case by case.

Secondly, just providing security should not be the only thing we should think of. We should think about how their future can be safeguarded. We should make sure that they have self-determination. They should have a right to make a choice for their future.

And we took steps to it. Education was the main focus—how do we create bi-cultural and bi-lingual system for all communities in different parts of the forest? It should not be that we expect them to go to school, but the school should go to them because they are forest communities that live in different parts of the forests at different times.

We created curriculum, programmes, and even erected schools in the forest in different locations. For the first time, we created textbooks in Jarawa so that people could teach the Jarawa kids Hindi while themselves also learning Jarawa. If tomorrow the Jarawa have to come to Port Blair to make their Aadhaar Card, they should be able to do that, rather than depending on someone else. But then they should be able to go back to their forest and continue doing their own traditions. So that maybe a few years later they can say we are making a cooperative of honey from our own forest.

Q. How did the administration respond to these steps?

There were some supportive people on the top who allowed for things to happen in a constructive way. But slowly the administration also started saying that all this is not needed, give the tribals roti kapda makaan (food, clothes and housing) and that will keep them quiet.

We got the administration to agree to give extra allowance to the welfare workers to teach the classes for Jarawas. We gave them training on how to use the textbooks created for them.

But a lot of work also got restricted during Covid when there were restrictions of entering the tribal territories to protect the communities themselves. Now, the school buildings have all collapsed.

Q. Does ANTRI still exist?

The building and the museum we created are still there, but they are locked up. The Andaman Adim Janjati Vikas Samiti is a trust that is supposed to look after all the tribal communities. Therefore, they are bound by rules of the Samiti to hold meetings and give account of what expenditure has been done and where it will be done in the future. Why are these meetings not held? It's taxpayers' money. It's people's right.

Q. Do you see anything strikingly different about the upcoming Nicobar project?

In many ways it's like history repeating itself again. The impact of this kind of policy we have already seen with Jarawas. The road that was built through the Jarawa reserve created a nasty problem.

(First published as 'Releasing Nicobar report would be like "opening can of worms" says anthropologist Vishvajit Pandya', in *Scroll.in*, 7 January 2025.)

15

Bolstering Security Without Ecological Harm

Is the huge investment in a transshipment port and other infrastructure on the Great Nicobar Island really needed to bolster India's strategic presence in the region? Or would a lighter touch with the reinforcing of current defence facilities have been enough?

Admiral Arun Prakash believes that a lighter touch would have worked just as well. Admiral Prakash, now retired and living in Goa, is a former Navy Chief. He was head of the joint command of the Army, Navy, Air Force and Coast Guard in the Andaman and Nicobar Islands.

Admiral Prakash says strengthening of India's presence is needed. But it could be achieved by merely expanding India's defence capabilities on the Great Nicobar and also using some of the smaller islands, if required. In this way, there wouldn't be the

Bolstering Security Without Ecological Harm

ecological damage that is going to be caused by large commercial facilities.

Q. Can you tell our readers why the islands are of great strategic significance and suddenly an urgent national security issue?

My connection to the islands goes back to 2001, when I was posted as Commander-in-Chief of the newly formed Andaman and Nicobar Command. Till then, the islands had been looked after by the Navy. Fortress Andaman Nicobar, located there, was manned by only the Navy, with small elements of the Air Force and Army made available.

After the 1999 Kargil War, a major defence review took place, and one of its outcomes was that the Government of India decided to bolster the security of the Andaman and Nicobar Islands. To this end, it was decided to create a joint command in the Andaman and Nicobar Islands, with a Commander-in-Chief who would have under his command elements of the services—the Army, Navy, Air Force, as well as the Coast Guard.

The Andaman and Nicobar archipelago, as we know, is strategically located in the middle of the Bay of Bengal, almost equidistant between the Indian peninsula and Southeast Asia. Myanmar and Thailand are quite close, and the northern tip of Indonesia is just about 90 miles from the southernmost island, which is Great Nicobar Island.

Given this location, and the fact that the Andaman and Nicobar archipelago dominates the shipping lanes which run from the Pacific, through the Strait of Malacca, across the Indian Ocean to the Persian Gulf, the Red Sea, and then on to Europe, it occupies a very strategic position.

If we go back into history, the Japanese, within weeks of the Pearl Harbor attack (in December 1941), swept across Southeast Asia and by March 1942, they had occupied the Andaman and Nicobar Islands, chasing out the British garrison. Having established their headquarter in Port Blair, they were going to use the islands as the springboard for their invasion of India, which never came about.

Then, we come to the time of Independence. Pakistan's Mohammad Ali Jinnah made a bid for these islands, basing his claim on the fact that they lay on the sea route from West Pakistan to East Pakistan. At the same time, the UK Chiefs of Staff told their government that these islands were of strategic value to British interests in the East, and should be retained as Crown possessions. I think we should consider it fortunate that, for various reasons, the British agreed to oblige Nehru, and handed over the islands to India.

I gave this background to highlight the strategic importance of these islands to India, and why we cannot afford to neglect them. They can be a springboard for India to implement whatever policy initiatives it wants in the strategic sphere. On the other hand, if they fall into the hands of an adversary power, they can pose a huge threat to India. Their strategic importance to India is increasing by the day—given the emergence of China and the Indo-Pacific paradigm.

Q. Despite the fact that we have remained in control of the islands, is our possession of them inadequate?

Well, it is not inadequate but it needs to be reinforced. The archipelago spans 700 to 800 miles, north to south, but since most of the islands are uninhabited, it is up to us to bolster our presence so that our possession of the islands cannot be challenged. At this moment, we are there, our forces are there, the islands seem well protected, but who can predict the future?

Q. What would be the advantage of this huge project which we are undertaking on the Great Nicobar Island? What is the strategic value we gain from it?

The Great Nicobar Island is one of the largest islands in that chain and, as I pointed out, as the southernmost island it is closest to Indonesia and the Malacca Strait. This strait is the shortest, safest and most economical exit and entry point for all the shipping that traverses to and from the Pacific and Indian Oceans, carrying oil, energy, raw material and other trade.

If you create a military stronghold in the Great Nicobar then you can dominate the Malacca Strait very conspicuously. We already have a presence on this island, by way of a small airstrip, a naval air station, a minor port and a small garrison—all on the eastern side of the island. There is room to bolster, expand and reinforce the existing military presence and infrastructure. I would imagine that there is plenty of land or space available without significantly disturbing or disrupting any of the valuable ecological or anthropologic assets of the island.

And, secondly, if you still want more land for military infrastructure, there are other islands just north of Great Nicobar where you could accommodate an airfield and a port.

Q. What can be done to meet strategic objectives and still have a lighter touch on the environment?

If you're only thinking of bolstering your security capabilities, there is adequate space on the eastern part of the Great Nicobar. As I mentioned, the minor port in Campbell Bay, the existing airstrip and the army garrison all have room for expansion and extension to meet enhanced security requirements. There are also smaller islands to the north of the Great Nicobar which could accommodate airfields, harbours and garrisons.

Q. How imminent is the danger of China occupying these islands in military terms?

While it may have been a possibility a few decades ago, it is a far-fetched idea today. The nearest Chinese naval base, in Hainan, is about 3,000 miles away. Moreover, they've got many other problems at their doorstep that they need to worry about; like Taiwan, for instance. On the other hand, Deng Xiaoping admitted in 2003, soon after we formed the Andaman Nicobar Command, that China faced a 'Malacca dilemma'.

Deng coined this phrase because he felt that closing of the Malacca Strait by an adversary could form an 'iron chain around China's neck'. He was referring to the fact that almost 80 to 90 per cent of China's energy trade, raw materials, finished goods, etc., passes through the Malacca Strait. Any power which decides to interfere, interdict or choke off this area can cause immense damage to China's economy, industry, trade and so on.

So, it is China that should be worried about what happens in the Malacca Strait rather than us running scared of somebody coming and occupying the islands.

Q. Does our attempt to bolster our presence by having this extensive form of development on the Great Nicobar change the strategic environment in any way?

Of course it will. If you're going to spend Rs 72,000 crore in developing an island which is sitting at the mouth of the Malacca Strait, it's going to send a huge message and may even ring alarm bells in the region. It may possibly be resented in Indonesia, which is next door, or in Malaysia, because it spells 'competition' in many spheres. So, it is a very significant message, there is no doubt about it.

Q. But what should the priorities be for the development and ecology of the islands? Or is defence the single biggest priority?

When I was the Commander-in-Chief, all these issues were of concern. But they needed to be looked at in three separate boxes. One was the welfare of the islanders, because the economy is, as you know, very minimal. They live mostly on support from the mainland. There is a need to develop the islands so that they can become as self-sustaining as possible and people can earn a living on their own.

It was quite apparent that there were two main areas in which the economy could be expanded on a sustainable basis—tourism and fisheries. The islands have a huge exclusive economic zone where our fishermen are seen occasionally, but neighbours' trawlers come in and take away a huge catch. We hardly have any fishing initiatives on an industrial scale, just small trawlers and little canoes, etc.

The other was the ecology. Many of the islands are in a pristine state. You have tribes that have lived there continuously for millennia—unspoilt by 'civilisation'. This is very precious heritage which we need to protect and preserve for as long as possible.

And the third factor was security. In which order of priority you consider these three depends on who you are. As Commander-in-Chief, security came first for me. At that point of time (2001–03), we had put forward a plan which ensured that we had a military 'presence' from north to south with adequate forces to deter and, if required, arrest foreign trespassers, poachers and illegal fishermen. While some of our proposals did receive approval, many requirements remained unfulfilled due to the internal dynamics of the service headquarters.

However, much has changed since and now one understands that there is a security presence right across the islands. From north to south, there's a Naval Air Base in Diglipur, close to Myanmar; then, in the middle, there is a Naval Base and Naval Air Base as well as Army presence in Port Blair; further south we have Car Nicobar which is an Air Force Station; and finally, in the south, there is Great Nicobar, which I have already described. The current presence can be built upon and bolstered by inducting more units, more firepower as well as sensors like radars, etc.

Is there any conflict between ecology and security? This is not really within my purview but I would say that if there is a conflict, there is enough room to accommodate all concerns and achieve a balance.

Q. In purely commercial terms, do you see a large port over there being viable?

I'm not an expert so I'm not going to claim any great depth of knowledge here. However, common sense tells me that in the vicinity of the Great Nicobar, there are ports like Singapore, Port Klang in Malaysia, and Hambantota, created by the Chinese for Sri Lanka. A little farther on is the large port of Colombo. All these ports constitute what are called 'transshipment ports' for India.

This is because most Indian ports are unable to cope with large container-carrying ships. So right now most container traffic destined for Indian ports is offloaded in one of these transshipment ports. Smaller ships which can dock in Indian ports pick up goods from these ports and bring them to India.

The ports I mention are old, established transshipment ports. Very recently, we've also proudly inaugurated Vizhinjam Port in

Kerala, touted as the first Indian transshipment port, which is meant to take away traffic from Colombo Port.

To my mind, given the close proximity of these ports, it will take considerable time for a new port like Great Nicobar to establish itself, and begin taking away traffic from these ports. I'm sure experts have examined this issue but, to my mind, I would say that it will take time for a new port to be able to compete with existing ports which have been around for many years and are very efficient.

Secondly, a major port in Great Nicobar will lack a hinterland. I am not familiar with the proposed master plan, but currently the rest of the island is just tropical jungle, tribals, crocodiles and the Galathea River. Let's remember the geographic remoteness of Great Nicobar. It is 1,000 km from Chennai, 2,000 km from Kolkata. It would be a matter of time, perhaps several decades, before such a port becomes established. It can happen, but it will take time and a major struggle before it can become a reality.

(First published as 'Possible to bolster security without harming ecology', in *Civil Society*, 28 December 2024.)

AFTERWORD

16

A Port of No Return[1]

Pankaj Sekhsaria

Imagine a large patch of low-lying land on the outskirts of any of our ever-expanding metros. Though registered in government records as a lake, it has been dry for a few years because of poor rains. By a sleight of hand well-known to the Indian public, the land is taken over by a builder, a high-rise is constructed in double quick time and occupants move in with much fanfare. The rains return, land becomes lake and the residents are marooned. The aggrieved home-owners go to court, which in turn asks the government to fix responsibility. The government sets up an enquiry committee which comes back with an ingenious solution: the lake that was a lake till recently was never a lake in the first place. And now that there is a building here how can this be a lake anyway? If migratory birds were visiting, it was their illusion that this was a lake, and the bird sanctuary here had been denotified many years ago anyway.

A farce—or should we call it subterfuge?—much bigger than this has just been played out in the Great Nicobar Island. At the heart of the matter are two related aspects: first, a category of land labelled by Indian law as coastal regulation zone (CRZ-1A) and second, the environmental clearance granted by the Ministry of Environment, Forest and Climate Change (MoEFCC) to a Rs 42,000 crore transshipment port in Great Nicobar Island's Galathea Bay. Coastal areas that are notified as protected areas (wildlife sanctuary and national park), with mangroves, corals, turtle-nesting beaches, sea grass beds and nesting grounds of birds, among others, are included in CRZ-1A. Significantly, they are out of bounds for large construction projects such as the port in question in Great Nicobar Island.

The beach at Galathea Bay, the site of the proposed port, is one of the most significant nesting sites in the Indian Ocean of the giant leatherback, the world's largest sea turtle, in addition to three other species that also nest here. The project site also has coral colonies and mangroves as mentioned in the project's Environment Impact Assessment report, and the adjoining coastal forests have important nesting sites of the endemic Nicobar megapode. It was to conserve this richness and diversity that Galathea Bay was proposed in 1997 as a wildlife sanctuary over 11 square kilometres of sea, coast and coastal forest. This was clearly CRZ-1A and a port was out of the question here.

But the path was cleared, first and foremost, by denotifying the sanctuary in January 2021 even though the turtles continue nesting here. Galathea Bay Wildlife Sanctuary should never have been denotified, the MoEFCC's Environment Appraisal Committee (EAC) should never have recommended the project for clearance and the MoEFCC should never have cleared the project that it did in November 2022. This was then challenged in the National Green Tribunal (NGT), which even as it failed its mandate spectacularly, could not help but note that the project site had 20,668 coral colonies and 'that part of the project is in CRZ-IA area where Port is prohibited.'

Table 3a: Status of Leatherback turtle nests at the important beaches/bays of the Great Nicobar.

Year	Anderson Bay	Vijay Nagar	Laxmi Nagar	Gandhi Nagar	Shastri Nagar	Galathea Bay	Pemayya Bay	Alexandria Bay	Casuarina Bay
1991-92	-	-	-	-	-	158	-	343	171
2000-01	-	-	-	-	-	524	-	866	362
2015-16	-	-	1	-	-	412	-	66	166
2016-17	4	-	0	-	4	90	-	-	-
2017-18	4	-	0	-	0	182	-	-	-
2018-19	4	-	1	-	0	203	-	-	-

Source: WII report, 2022

Table 3b: Number of leatherback nestings on the beaches of Great Nicobar from 2022-2024

Beach	2022	2023	2024
Govindnagar	6	3	15
Laxminagar	0	0	4
Shastrinagar	0	0	0
Galathea	649	505	619

Source: RTI reply from Andaman Nicobar Forest Department

The NGT then appointed a high-powered committee (HPC) headed by the Secretary, MoEFCC, with a key member being the Chief Secretary (CS), Andaman and Nicobar Islands, to look into the matter. It did not strike the NGT that the CS is the chairman of the board of directors of the Andaman & Nicobar Islands Integrated Development Corporation Limited (ANIIDCO), the project proponent whose environmental clearance was under question or that the MoEFCC was the very agency that had granted this clearance. They would be sitting now in judgement on a challenge to their own actions.

The problem, however, remained unresolved because the project site was still CRZ-1A based on scientific records, in reports of the Andaman and Nicobar Coastal Zone Management Authority and the National Centre for Sustainable Coastal Management (NCSCM) and, indeed, the order of the NGT constituting the HPC. A port still could not be allowed and a solution was still needed. The workaround came via a ground truthing survey the NCSCM is supposed to have conducted recently. Read carefully the following from ANIIDCO's affidavit in the NGT that was also the basis of the *Indian Express* report: 'The HPC came to the conclusion that in the Report submitted by the NCSCM, it has been determined that construction of port is permissible in CRZ-IB area but not permissible in CRZ-1A. The NCSCM, hence, concluded that no part of the project area is falling under CRZ-1A.'

The turtles still nest here, the mangroves still stand, the megapodes still forage and breed here and 20,688 coral colonies still flourish in the adjoining waters. This is still CRZ-1A, but now that the port has been approved, this cannot be 1A. It should never have been 1A in the first place. The cart was unfortunately before the horse all along but this has been corrected now.

And there is more.

Money for Ecological Studies

In early 2025, two years after the grant of environment and forest clearances, and a few months after change of the CRZ category, ANIIDCO released details of meetings held to discuss implementation of environmental conditions under which the project was cleared. Rs 9,162 crore are to be spent over thirty years for the 'environment management plan for wildlife, compensatory afforestation, tribal welfare and conservation and mitigation measures during construction and operation of the project.'

Of this amount, Rs 2,220 crore, or nearly 25 per cent, is for the conservation plans for different species and ecosystems by institutions that include the Salim Ali Centre for Ornithology and Natural History (SACON), Coimbatore, Wildlife Institute of India (WII), Dehradun, Indian Institute of Forest Management, Bhopal, the Zoological and Botanical Surveys of India (ZSI and BSI), and the Andaman and Nicobar Forest Department (ANFD). On the surface, Rs 2,220 crore would seem a very large amount, and perhaps welcome too.

Table 4: Budget for wildlife conservation and tribal welfare plans and special medical unit

Sl. No.	Institution	Component	Project Duration (in years)	Cost (in INR crores) First 5 Years	Total
1.	WII, ZSI, SACON, BSI, IIFM, A&NFD	Wildlife conservation plans for Leatherback Sea Turtles, Nicobar Megapode, Saltwater Crocodile, Nicobar Macaque, Mangrove Restoration, Corals etc.	30	326.23	2220.41
2.	Department of Tribal Welfare (DTW)	Detailed proposal for welfare, wellbeing and safety of tribes of Great Nicobar Island	50	37.03	75.0
3.	Directorate of Health Services (DHS)	Proposal for the development of health care infrastructure under Great Nicobar project for setting up of special medical and health care unit for prevention and control of diseases with special reference to tribal populations.	10	42.08	126.98

Source: Minutes of 'Monitoring Committee Meeting–Implementation of EMP for Development of Green Field Airport' ANIIDCO, 14 November 2024

The problem, however, lies in the fact that those getting this money are the very institutions—WII, ZSI and the ANFD—that facilitated the wildlife and environment clearances in the first place. The ZSI, which did an important part of the assessment report leading up to the environment clearance and was also part of the NGT-appointed high-powered committee that dismissed a host of environmental concerns stands to gain funding of more than Rs 1,000 crore over thirty years for three projects it will execute. The ANFD that has agreed to hand over large areas of pristine forest and biodiversity-rich habitat for the project now stands to receive Rs 72 crore for work on two projects.

The case of WII, considered India's premier wildlife research institute, is particularly illustrative—and heart-breaking. It is linked to Galathea Bay in Great Nicobar Island, a very important nesting for four marine turtle species, including the giant leatherback. More than four hundred leatherback nestings are recorded annually at Galathea Bay, making this one of its most important nesting sites in the northern Indian Ocean. India's National Marine Turtle Action Plan, released in January 2021, too listed Galathea Bay as one of the country's most important turtle nesting beaches; 11.44 square kilometres of the bay, including the beaches there, had in fact been declared a wildlife sanctuary in 1997 for conserving precisely this unique system and its rare inhabitants.

And then it was decided that Galathea Bay will be the site for the transshipment port, the centrepiece of the now Rs 81,000 crore mega-infra project. The sanctuary would have to go and the denotification was facilitated with minimum fuss in the sixtieth meeting of the standing committee of the National Board for Wildlife, held in January 2021. In attendance as an important member was the then Director of the WII, Dhananjai Mohan. Not only did he not oppose the denotification but opined that 'the concerned authorities develop and implement a mitigation plan to facilitate leatherback and other turtles to continuously nest (...) *near* (emphasis added) the Galathea Bay.' He concurred further that 'the preservation and conservation of the leatherback turtle habitat will not be compromised even if the area is de-notified.'

This is impossible and defies logic given that the port design itself proposes to close the mouth of Galathea Bay by 90 per cent—from the current 3 kilometres to a mere 300 metres to ensure passage for shipping. The turtles might not be able to even reach the beach anymore, leave alone complete their nesting activities. In a shocking response to an RTI query a few months later, the WII admitted it had never conducted any study ever on the leatherback turtles in the Andaman and Nicobar Islands.

It is the same WII that has now put together three proposals for a cumulative amount of Rs 391.52 crore for management and conservation of wildlife here. The single largest component, of Rs 237.45 crore, is ironically, and tragically, for the 'conservation and long-term monitoring of leatherback sea turtle'. The actual money that will flow into the coffers of the WII is actually much more. Added to its Rs 391.52 crore will be another Rs 376.46 crore for the seven proposals put in by SACON, which was merged with the WII in 2023.

The WII that has never worked on sea turtles in these islands was allowed to sign away one of the world's most important turtle nesting sites that it knows nothing about. They stand to now get funding to the tune of Rs 768 crores for thirty years. At Rs 25 crore per year, this is already 50 per cent of the Rs 52.32 crore allocated for the institute in the latest Union budget.

One might never have imagined that one clearance could lead to such substantial benefits. A question about this is surely a legitimate one to ask.

17

The Human Cost of Misgovernance

M. Rajshekhar

Do islands need ships? At least one island administration—the one running Andaman and Nicobar Islands—doesn't think so.

In 2016, it ordered four ships from Cochin Shipyard. Two of these, capable of lugging 500 passengers and 150 tons of cargo, were to ply within the archipelago. The other two, with an intake of 1,200 passengers and 1,000 tons of cargo, were to run between the mainland and Sri Vijaya Puram, as Port Blair has been freshly rechristened.

Work began. The first of these ships, *MV Ashoka*, was 'on track for delivery' by the end of 2021. By August 2022, the second ship, *MV Atal*, was ready as well, and had to be outfitted with machinery and living quarters.

Payments from the administration had moved smoothly as well. Of the Rs 1,294 crore it had to pay Cochin Shipyard, Rs 819.22

crore were meant for *Atal* and *Ashoka*. By June 2023, sticking to the payment schedule, the administration had transferred 80 per cent of this amount.

By June, however, the Andaman administration had dropped a bomb. It didn't want the ships.

The travel habits of the locals have changed, an unnamed official in the administration told *Economic Times*. 'The island people who were totally dependent on water transport to travel to the mainland and back, are now increasingly using air transport for their travel needs, saving the 2-3 days required for journey by ship one way, as cheaper air tickets aided by government schemes force a change in their travel patterns,' the business paper wrote, quoting the official.

It was an extraordinary assertion. Not only had the administration backed away from ships it had already paid for, it was also ignoring island realities. 'We had three ships—Nancowry, Nicobar and Swaraj Deep—that could carry 1,200 passengers,' an official in the administration's Directorate of Shipping told this reporter. 'Given a large earthquake, roads and runways will crack. These ships were very useful during emergencies. During the tsunami, these ships had been working heavily.'

Even in normal times, these ships are a critical lifeline. India's Ministry of Ports, Shipping and Waterways doesn't reveal passenger numbers for specific routes like Chennai/Kolkata/Vizag to Port Blair but the Directorate of Shipping official pegged *Swaraj Dweep*'s capacity utilisation at 150–300 passengers in the off-season and 1,200 in the peak season. These numbers, however, are despite the ship's poor maintenance. And then, there is cargo. 'Vegetables for Andaman and Nicobar come from Chennai or Kolkata,' said the official. 'Right now, we are getting potatoes at Rs 100 a kilo because the supply is not very good. If we have these big ships, all those transport problems would be taken care of.'

In addition, while ships do take two to three days to reach the mainland, they are cheaper and an alternative mode of transport. In peak season or at short notice, air tickets are either unavailable or they cost the earth—with prices above Rs 20,000, a hard ask for any islander family that needs to rush to the mainland. In contrast, a bunk in the ships between Port Blair and Chennai costs Rs 1,300 for islanders.

Despite such counterarguments, the Andaman and Nicobar Administration refused to yield. It suggested the Navy take these ships—a proposal opposed by the islands' former MP. Thereafter, Cochin Shipyard tried selling these ships to Lakshadweep. That proposal, too, went nowhere. According to Vesselfinder, both ships are now plying under unknown flags. It's unclear if the Andaman administration recovered the Rs 819.22 crore it had paid Cochin Shipyard. The *News Minute* posed this question to Andaman and Nicobar Lieutenant Governor D.K. Joshi and Chief Secretary Chandra Bhushan Kumar. No response has been received so far.

Clearer, though, are the fallouts for islanders. Of the three large 1,200 seater ships plying between the mainland and the islands—*MV Nancowry*, *MV Nicobar* and *MV Swaraj Dweep*—just one is left. 'Nancowry and Nicobar have already been condemned,' said the official. 'In two years, *Swaraj Dweep* will be decommissioned as well. Once that happens, we will not have any big vessels. We will have to turn to private charters.'

This decision on *MV Atal* and *MV Ashoka*—which militates against islanders' welfare—is not an isolated instance.

In recent years, the Andaman and Nicobar administration has also taken away panchayats' power for local expenditure, underfunded healthcare, steamrolled projects like the Great Nicobar transhipment port despite objections from local communities, ignored local demands for industry-friendly policy, used transfers as a punitive measure to ensure compliance, hurt the islands' indigenous people, one could go on. Put all these patterns together and you will see some central traits of the current Andaman and Nicobar administration its inability to think like islanders, a wilful under-provisioning of services to the locals, recklessness with public finances and an unwillingness to engage with local demands. These traits raise concerns about how the government's new infrastructure push on the islands will play out in practice.

Shadow of Misgovernance

Hardwired into these decisions is a larger regression in the UT administration. The archipelago has little independent media, civil society or centres of political power, an arrangement which concentrates powers with bureaucrats, overseen only by the Lieutenant Governor, the Chief Secretary and the Ministry of Home Affairs. In the past too, ergo, its administration has faced local flak for misgovernance and an obliviousness to island realities—like the insistence on building roads over investing in ships.

Even with that backdrop, what the islanders are seeing today is new. The UT administration is tilting even further in favour of itself, outsiders and large construction projects over the islanders—with a corresponding rise in intolerance towards criticism.

This drift has not received the attention it deserves. Like Lakshadweep, Andaman and Nicobar rarely make it to national headlines. Only eye-popping developments—like the tsunami of 2004, rape charges against a former Chief Secretary, or plans to build a transhipment port at Great Nicobar—get reported by the media. More local developments do not get the attention they deserve.

And yet, unlike the mainland, misgovernance casts a longer shadow on the islands. Given low population, few resources and geographic isolation, people here rely on the administration for basic needs like travel, employment, healthcare and housing. When the administration turns truant, islanders' lives get severely circumscribed.

Healthcare Takes a Back Seat

From outside, the primary health centre (PHC) at Campbell Bay looks adequate. It's a single-storeyed structure which calls old government schools to mind—with rooms with asbestos sheet roofs lining a rectangular central courtyard.

On stepping inside, the initial perception starts to fade. Despite getting 120 to 150 patients a day, it has just two allopaths and a dentist, apart from one ayurvedic doctor and one homeopath. Despite locals still carrying scars from the 2004 tsunami, it doesn't have mental health specialists. It has an X-ray machine but no facility for ultrasound scans. Cows and wander dogs stray into hospital premises. As recently as 2020, patients in the general ward and the TB ward shared a common toilet.

That is just the start. This PHC is the apex health centre for all of Great Nicobar which has a population of just over 8,000 people. Patients it cannot handle have to travel 523 kilometres to Port Blair. This is easier said than done. Connectivity between Port Blair and Campbell Bay is erratic. The *MV Sindhu*, the sole ship between these two administrative centres, comes once a week. There is air connectivity, but between inclement weather, three-seater helicopters and ten-seater dorniers which also have to accommodate VIPs and passengers from Car Nicobar, flight seats are not always available. At Rs 5,350 per seat, they are also expensive.

Most households in Campbell Bay, a resident told the *News Minute*, earn between Rs 1.5 lakh to Rs 2 lakh a year—a monthly income of Rs 12,500 to Rs 16,600. Flights, ergo, used to be free for patients till three years ago. 'But, for the last three years, both patients and nurses accompanying them have had to pay,' said a medical worker in the archipelago on the condition of anonymity.

For all these reasons, locals have been asking the administration to upgrade the PHC to a community health centre (CHC). 'If it becomes a CHC, the centre will have a surgeon and a gynaecologist,' said the medical worker. 'Campbell Bay can take care of patients here instead of sending them to Port Blair.' The hospital, added the medical worker, also needs to separate its TB ward from the rest of the hospital. In spite of all these reasons, the administration has not upgraded the PHC. 'The administration says Campbell Bay's population is very low—just 8,367 in the 2011 Census—and so, it qualifies only for a PHC,' said the worker.

As responses go, this one is odd. The total population of Andaman and Nicobar is about 7 lakh, which makes it one of India's smallest districts. Extending that logic, the archipelago should be governed by just one District Collector. Instead, it has a veritable buffet of administrators—apart from the Lieutenant Governor (LG) and the Chief Secretary (CS), the archipelago has seventeen IAS officers and twenty-three DANICS officers.

At the PHC, there are other signs of administrative apathy. Its building needs to be overhauled. Staff quarters too are in disrepair. 'A full renovation of the PHC will cost Rs 3 crore,' said the medical worker. 'This has been shot down each year saying the expenditure is too high.'

The administration, however, has spent Rs 819.22 crore on *MV Atal* and *MV Ashoka*.

Campbell Bay is not an exception. In Hut Bay (Little Andaman) too, there is no doctor for the ultrasound machine, forcing patients to travel to Port Blair for scans. Earlier this month, when chopper tickets weren't available, an eighty-two-year-old diabetic heart

> Despite a budget allocation of Rs 6,212.06 crore for 2025-26, the Andaman and Nicobar Islands administration spends nearly half on its own salaries and maintenance, while sectors like public health and disaster management receive a fraction.
>
> Of the total budget, Rs 3,100.86 crore is allocated for administrative maintenance and salaries, Rs 18.13 crore for disaster management, Rs 99.92 crore for rural development and Rs 133.59 crore for medical and public health.
>
> *Source*: Note on Demand for Grants, 2025-26

patient had to endure a ten-hour ship journey from Diglipur to Port Blair. In Car Nicobar, there is a dialysis unit but no technician. In Port Blair itself, the leading government hospital doesn't have MRI facilities. 'Patients have to go to a private hospital for scans,' a businessman in Port Blair told the *News Minute*.

It gets worse. 'Earlier, specialists like ENTs used to go to the far islands like Car Nicobar,' said the businessman. 'That has been discontinued as well.'

The *News Minute* wrote to LG Joshi and CS Kumar asking them to explain these decisions. No response has been received for this so far.

On the whole, NFHS-5 data suggests infant and under-five mortality rates, an indicator for community health, have risen between 2015-16 and 2019-20 (IMR from 9.8 to 20.6; child mortality from 13 to 24.5).

This, however, is just one instance. Elsewhere in the islands too, hideous misgovernance shows up.

Marginalisation Threatens Indigenous Communities

The map by Chandi makes for sombre reading (see Map 3).

A pre-tsunami sketch of Great Nicobar, it shows where close to fifty villages of the tribal community of the Nicobarese stood on the island. As books like Simron Jit Singh's *In The Sea of Influence* describe, these communities were self-sufficient with distinctive cosmologies and community structures.

'The plantations were the commons,' said one tribal elder. 'People used to take turns to make copra.'

Then came the tsunami.

The worst impacts were felt in the Nicobars. Trinkat broke into four pieces. Waves crossed Katchal and rejoined the sea on the other side. In Car Nicobar, as many as 2,000 people died. Such was the quake that the archipelago itself tilted. Great Nicobar dipped, pulling the lighthouse at Indira Point into the sea, while North Andaman rose, pushing coral reefs off Diglipur above the waterline.

What happened thereafter is well-known. Six of the twelve inhabited islands in the Nicobars were entirely evacuated. 'Nearly 29,000 survivors, both Nicobarese (roughly 20,000) and non-Nicobarese, were relocated to 118 relief camps across Car Nicobar, Nancowry, Kamorta, Katchal, Teressa, and Great Nicobar,' wrote Ajay Saini in his 28 December 2024 article in *Frontline* titled 'How Tsunami Aid Triggered a Social Disaster in Nicobar'. By mid-2005, temporary tin shelters were erected for the displaced Nicobarese, where they received basic amenities, rations, relief supplies and financial assistance.

On Great Nicobar, most of these villages ceased to exist. The number of families, estimated at 400 by a tribal elder before the tsunami, fell below a hundred. Survivors were moved to three settlements—Afra Bay in the north, Rajiv Nagar in Campbell Bay, and New Chingenh near Joginder Nagar.

What happened thereafter is staggering. Even twenty years after the tsunami, these survivors have not been allowed to return to their villages. The Nicobarese wanted to. 'That is a good place for us,' said a tribal elder in Campbell Bay. 'We can have our plantations of supari (areca nut) and nariyal (coconut). There is also crab export that we can get into. We have been saying this to the administration but there is no response.'

The administration's defence pivots around expenditure, he said.

'They say: It's far. There is no road. It is not easy to provide medical and schools in the villages. Which is why we shifted you here. If there is a tsunami again, how will we take care of you.'

These are odd responses. Take Chingenh. This village of 100–150 houses, located just to the east of Galathea Bay, had a primary and middle school before the tsunami. 'It was a big basti (settlement),' said a local. 'Buses ran till six in the evening. If these were possible then, why not now?' Similarly, if the administration is worried about another destructive tsunami, why is it building the transhipment port at Galathea?

Even as the administration barred the Nicobarese from moving back, it did not help these communities recover from the tsunami. At both Chingenh and Rajiv Nagar, locals asked for nearby land on which they could set up plantations. They didn't get any. As a result, in both Rajiv Nagar and New Chingenh, survivors are working as daily rated mazdoors (DRMs) or contract labour. 'They have been forced to move from a plantation economy to a finance economy,' said anthropologist Anstice Justin. 'They used to grow arecanuts, coconuts, vegetables and edible roots in plantations and village gardens. Now they have been pushed into wage work.'

Coming with deep social and cultural losses, such shifts amount to ethnocide. Without plantations, the Nicobarese no longer have room or raw materials for their traditional functions. 'A ceremony that used to take a week now gets done in a day. We do not have the samagri (materials),' said a tribal elder. This point is also made in a letter from the Tribal Council to the Andaman and Nicobar administration. 'Every activity (our customs and economic practices) we conduct through our traditional livelihoods are intricately connected to our erstwhile homes/villages that govern and "construct" our tribal identity,' says one letter written in 2022. 'This important aspect of our right to self-determination and choices for livelihood is missing in our current dwellings and circumstances.' In tandem, with shelters built for nuclear families, old joint family structures, as detailed by Singh in his book, have been decimated as well. 'Families have all broken up,' said one elder in Rajiv Nagar. 'Our children have not seen Nicobarese culture.'

Proximity to mainland settlers has been a variable here, he said. 'In places like Afra Bay and Makachua to the north, tribals are doing a better job of persisting with our traditions.' Even there, however, there are problems. Two of their islands with plantations and spiritual significance, Menchal and Meroe, have been summarily turned into wildlife sanctuaries, without informing the tribal councils in time and despite the tribal council subsequently opposing the decision—and despite a lack of clarity if these islands are large enough to support the translocated species. Meroe, for instance, is just 1.29 square kilometres in size.

The *News Minute* wrote to LG Joshi and CS Kumar asking them to explain these decisions. No answer has been received in response thus far.

On yet another front—that of the economy—the administration is dragging its feet.

Land conversion—which lets locals repurpose farmland for housing, or residential land for commercial uses—is one instance. 'Land conversions used to be handled by local SDMs,' said the head of a business family in Port Blair on the condition of anonymity. 'About eight to ten years ago, after allegations of corruption, the administration took over those powers saying it will create a new system.' Accordingly, in around 2020, a new committee, with the Chief Secretary amongst the members, was set up.

What happened next is instructive. One, the idea of the committee was bad in law. 'The Andaman and Nicobar Land Revenue and Land Reforms Act and Rules says land conversions have to be approved by the Sub-Divisional Officer,' said the head of the business family. 'The idea of the committee is unsupported by existing law.'

Groups like industry associations went to the High Court and then the Supreme Court and got orders in their favour. The administration, however, has neither returned to the old system nor held any meetings of the Committee. 'In effect, there is no policy,' said the business family head. 'This has stopped any growth. Firms like Westside and KFC, which want to set up outlets, are not finding clear land. Indian Oil Corporation, which wants to set up petrol pumps, is not finding land either. Settlers cannot build a house on their own farmland. All the money which could come into the local economy because of construction is stuck.'

At the same time, however, the administration is converting government land for firms participating in its tourism bids. 'Over the last five years, the administration has been trying to get investors for 4 and 5 star hotels,' said the business family head. 'In the first set, there are four islands—Neil, Long, Avis, Ross and Smith. Thereafter, another eleven islands will be given out. This project, which was first under NITI Aayog, has now been taken over by ANIIDCO again.' For these, he said, the administration is converting government land and giving it on a platter to private companies.

Bid conditions, however, are such that local firms will struggle to participate in these tenders. 'The financial eligibility is Rs 100–200 crore. Technical expertise is five years' experience in running 5 star hotels. Given such terms, locals will not qualify.'

This pattern—of posting tenders too large for locals—extends beyond administrative centres to touch even villages. 'In the past, panchayats had the power to issue tenders up to Rs 6 lakh,' a resident of Campbell Bay, the administrative centre of Great Nicobar, told the *News Minute*. Proposals for small civil works—like minor road repairs—went to the Gram Sabha. Once approved, assistant engineers would see the fund availability certificate and then approve the works. If funds were available, the work would be bidded out to local societies—each run by a group of eleven locals each. 'This was another form of income for us,' said the villager. 'Average annual incomes here are low. And so, when we take a project from the panchayat, we will be left with a profit of Rs 30,000–Rs 40,000. This sum would be shared within the society members.'

Take Campbell Bay. It has three panchayats—Campbell Bay, Laxminagar and Govind Nagar—and, within those, about thirty-two societies. With each panchayat issuing three or four such projects each year, that worked out to a local expenditure of Rs 45 lakh to Rs 60 lakh—and about Rs 9 lakh to Rs 12 lakh in retained earnings for the locals. '*Chota mota kaam isse hota tha* (local jobwork was done with these funds),' said an official in the Campbell Bay panchayat office.

This system has now been done away with. In 2024, the administration took away 'cheque power', said the official in the Campbell Bay panchayat office. 'All tenders are online now. The government says this will stop corruption. Now, all tenders have to be over Rs 6,00,000 and they have to be tendered.'

With that, incomes from local construction are now flowing to government contractors—some of whom also have political links with the BJP. In Campbell Bay, for instance, both Sanjay Singh and E.S. Rajesh, the past and current Pramukhs, belong to the BJP and are civil contractors.

In tandem, locals have found their lives disrupted in two ways. People earning from societies have been displaced. 'We have seven societies in Campbell Bay panchayat,' said the panchayat official. 'In all, seventy-seven families lived off this work.' The new system is also less responsive. 'The advantage of the old system was that work would get done within fifteen to twenty days,' a resident of Vijaynagar told this reporter. 'In the new system, there is no guarantee. *Chota mota kaam sab ruka huva hain* (small jobwork is at a standstill).'

Letters asking the UT administration to rethink, said the panchayat official, have not received any response. The *News Minute* wrote to LG Joshi and CS Kumar asking them to explain these decisions. No answer has been received in response thus far.

These instances—shipping, healthcare, post-tsunami rehabilitation of the Nicobarese and the denial of economic opportunities to locals—are just the tip of the proverbial iceberg. On a clutch of other fronts too, islanders—tribals and settlers alike—are struggling.

On Great Nicobar, the government's claims in the parliament notwithstanding, both the Nicobarese and the Shompen will be affected by the proposed port project. As the government works on plans for the western coast as well, the Nicobarese are worried about their ancestral lands being lost forever.

As for the Shompen, the hunter-gatherer tribe lives in the island's hinterland—with groups living across the island, from its top to Galathea Bay in the south. These groups in the south will be displaced by the project. 'If they are pushed north, they will come into conflict with other tribespeople,' said a researcher who has worked in the islands. As human activity rises on the islands, interactions between the Shompen and outsiders will rise as well.

As the Onge and the Great Andamanese show, such interactions can be ethnocidal. As books like Madhusree Mukherjee's *Land of the Naked People* show, the Jarawas were still trying to balance their traditional lives and the world outside. Over the last ten years, however, that tightrope walk has faltered. 'AAJVS is giving alcohol to the Jarawas,' said Justin. 'If you look at their teeth, they are red from betelnut. We are now seeing instances of cancer. They have a potbelly.' That is because, he said, the AAJVS is giving them edible oil and rice in return for crab as a currency.' The Jarawas, he said, are heading the Great Andamanese way.

As these anecdotes over shipping, healthcare and land conversion show, settlers are struggling as well. On Great Nicobar, as Campbell Bay gets subsumed into the project, most settlers will lose their land. As with the Nicobarese, the government doesn't want to give alternative land. 'The government says it doesn't have enough land and so people who lose 11 acres might get just 1 acre,' said a resident of Vijay Nagar, one of the villages affected by the proposed airport. 'My husband's family came here when there was nothing,' she said. 'After the tsunami, we went back twenty years. Just as we recovered, this airport has come. We spent all this time on the land and now they want to take it back.'

The project, however, is getting 130 square kilometres of the island.

Elsewhere in the archipelago, the water crisis continues to fester. The administrative decision to use biometric verification at ration shops in these remote islands is making it hard for locals to claim rations. Inter-island movement is in shambles. Flight tickets are hard to come by—and the ship schedule, given lack of ships, comes with large gaps. 'Anyone travelling from Great Nicobar to Car Nicobar will have to wait as long as a week at Nancowry before the next ship comes,' said a government employee stationed at Campbell Bay. 'People sail first to Port Blair and then take a ship back!'

This reporter wrote to the LG and the chief secretary asking them to comment. No answer has been received in response thus far.

There are many other fronts in which administration has moved with extraordinary speed.

The proposed port-city complex in Great Nicobar is one instance. Public hearings have been rushed through. Two wildlife sanctuaries—one for turtles and the other for the Nicobar megapode—have even been shifted from the project site at Galathea Bay to the island's western coast. As a forest officer who has served in Campbell Bay asked: 'Can protected areas be shifted? If animals don't go there, how did we declare a place as a wildlife sanctuary?'

More recently, even as wildlife researchers at WII and SACON seek two years to gauge the project's impact on the government's (randomly compiled) list of locally endemic species like the Nicobar macaque, megapode and saltwater crocodile that will be affected by the project, the Andaman and Nicobar Industrial Development Corporation (ANIIDCO), which is implementing the project under the supervision of the Ministry of Home Affairs, has nonetheless invited expressions of interest for logging. 'We are not being told when logging will start,' said a researcher working on the project. 'We are afraid the administration will tell us, in some months or maybe a year, that "Logging is starting. Capture what you can. Save what you can."'

New Colonialism?

In effect, the archipelago is being colonised all over again.

During colonialism and India's heady post-Independence decades, the tribals were pushed aside by the settlers. This process is playing out again now, with a clutch of bureaucrats and firms from the mainland marginalising not just the locals but also provincial capitalists.

Great Nicobar is not the only project coming up on the islands. There are also plans to set up a deepwater port in Diglipur—at least one firm, called Meinhardt Shipping from Singapore, has already made a presentation to the UT administration. There is also talk of creating a huge tourism centre at Hut Bay, not to mention plans to set up resorts on eleven islands. And then, there is Great Nicobar itself.

Little of this, however, has been discussed with the locals. 'The administration should at least talk to MPs and elected representatives,' said Tejasva Rao, organising secretary of the Congress in Port Blair. 'At this time, no one is being taken into consideration—not the tribals, not the business community, not elected leaders, not the locals.' This unaccountability extends beyond construction projects to bureaucratic privilege.

While at Port Blair, I heard about an IAS officers' two-day trip—with spouses—to Barren Island for which *MV Sindhu* had been pulled out of its regular sailing schedule. The ship works through the week. Leaving Port Blair on Tuesday morning, it reaches Campbell Bay on Wednesday afternoon or evening. Heading back the very next morning, it reaches Port Blair on Friday morning. On Saturday, it heads to Little Andaman, returning to Blair only on Monday. Despite this schedule and locals' reliance on the ship, at least two times last year, government officials commandeered the ship for weekend trips to Barren Island. 'The ship left Port Blair on Saturday and returned on Sunday,' said the business family head. 'This happened last year, under the previous Chief Secretary. On both weekends, Hut Bay didn't have a ship service.'

This reporter wrote to the LG and the chief secretary asking them to comment but no response has been received thus far.

I heard too about an Ahmedabad-based firm called Dineshchandra R. Agrawal Infracon which has bagged the tender to re-tarmac the airstrip at Car Nicobar. To create an additional landing space for its construction material, the firm has dumped sand inside the harbour to create a makeshift barge landing jetty. This is resulting in the harbour silting up—with ships unable to dock as before. This reporter haSEs seen letters written by the tribal council in 2022—and again in 2023—to the administration asking for relief.

When I met them in 2025, the problem remained unaddressed.

In tandem, the administration is getting more intolerant towards criticism. As this reporter has written elsewhere, it's trying to stop outsiders—even tourists—from visiting Campbell Bay even though the administrative centre of Great Nicobar is revenue land and, ergo, open to all Indians. A reporting team from the *News Minute* that reached the island—making the thirty-hour journey by ship—was followed and questioned by local police and Intelligence Bureau officers.

This intolerance extends to locals as well. The administration is quick to issue prohibitory orders to curb local protests.

'We cannot speak,' said the resident of Vijay Nagar. 'If we do, local politicians will make it hard for us.' Government employees too have been disciplined—through instruments like postings to the far islands. 'There is no media here and so, they behave like this,' said a mid-level bureaucrat who had been transferred to Campbell Bay, compelling him to leave his aged father alone in Port Blair. 'If they knew they could get filmed or their deeds could go public in some other way, they would act differently,' he said.

The outcome is striking. On one hand, the administration materially shapes locals' lives—their access to traditional lands, medical care, travel; and determines where they stay and how they earn. At the same time, it acts with extraordinary unaccountability, circumscribing locals' lives as well as announcing grandiose plans. Earlier this year, for instance, LG Joshi said a global medical hub will be developed on Little Andaman. This plan, however, sidesteps questions about the administration's current track record on healthcare delivery or why anyone unwell will fly to an island in the middle of the Bay of Bengal.

Given pervasive underdevelopment, however, locals end up pinning hopes on such announcements which, like the transhipment port, might eventually produce only EPC and logging booms.

In all, anger against the administration is rising. 'There is more anger now than there was five years ago,' said a Directorate of Shipping official, on the condition of anonymity.

(First published in *The News Minute*, 10 April 2025.)

ANNEXURES

Annexure 1

Chronicle of an 'Ecocide' Foretold

T.R. Shankar Raman

Like the famous novella *Chronicle of a Death Foretold*, by the Colombian writer and Nobel laureate Gabriel García Márquez, the slim and punchy little book, *The Great Nicobar Betrayal* augurs a coming death. The portentous subtitle, 'Pushing a Vulnerable Island Knowingly into Disaster', foreshadows the contents: a collection of essays and articles on the wonders of the island of Great Nicobar in the Indian Ocean and the impending tragedy of its developmental death. Here, the book declares, is a death about to unfold before our eyes. And this will be no ordinary death. It will be the death of over 130 square kilometres of some of the best-preserved tropical rainforests in the world. It will be the death of the most exuberant marine life and ecosystems our oceans have to offer. It will spell disaster for the vulnerable indigenous tribal islanders.

The stakes are high. In Great Nicobar, the union government and its think tank, NITI Aayog, have envisaged a giant project estimated to cost Rs 72,000 crore. The project involves the creation of a new transshipment port, a new international airport, a power station, a township that will occupy 160 square kilometres, and facilities to spur a surge in tourism. As the book tells us, all this will extract huge human and ecological costs. Great Nicobar is home to two highly vulnerable indigenous communities. The nomadic, forest-dwelling Shompen and the Nicobarese, who were internally displaced during the 2004 tsunami, stand to lose their traditional villages and territories to the project.

The island is a part of the Sundaland global biodiversity hotspot, containing relatively intact tropical rainforests that support a raft of endemic species, including numerous plants, herpetofauna, birds like the Nicobar megapode and mammals like the Nicobar tree shrew. While the clearing of forests and loss of over a million old-growth trees will wreak devastation on land, the loss of coral reefs, turtle nesting grounds, and beaches will impact the marine ecosystems around. The scale of the project is such that the foretold death of these ecosystems is better described by the word 'ecocide', indicating ecosystem destruction on a colossal scale.

A Deconstruction of Destruction

The first chapter titled 'The great misadaventure' presents an overview written by the scholar, writer, and activist, Pankaj Sekhsaria, who teaches at IIT Bombay and has written several earlier books and numerous articles based on his long familiarity with the Andaman and Nicobar Islands. Sekhsaria, who has also curated the set of chapters included in this book, describes the scale of the project and flags the wholly inadequate and hasty environmental impact assessment (EIA) and clearance process that has already set the wrecking ball rolling. He pinpoints the incongruity of the environment ministry's issuing in January 2021 a National Marine Turtle Action Plan that talks about conserving Galathea Bay, a nesting site for the endangered leatherback sea turtle, when the sanctuary that protected this very bay had been denotified just two weeks earlier to make way for the project.

In the next chapter, he goes on to assail the lack of transparency in the forest clearance process while bringing to the fore the sheer absurdity of the proposal to compensate for the destruction of the extraordinary rainforests of Great Nicobar by large-scale plantations of trees in distant Haryana in the dry Aravallis of northern India.

Shoddy and steam-rolled environmental clearance processes are not new in India's poor system of regulation that privileges 'development' and the claims of project proponents and agencies hired by them to generate largely favourable reports. But what makes the Great Nicobar project rather egregious in this aspect is that the EIA hardly considers the serious risks involved in a project of this nature in a seismically and volcanically-active region prone to earthquakes and tsunamis. This oversight is the subject of a chapter by Janki Andharia, a professor with the Centre for Disasters and Development at the Tata Institute of Social Sciences (TISS), Mumbai, and her colleagues. They draw attention to the '... possible damage and destruction of national property that could be caused by future earthquakes, volcanic eruptions, and tsunamis ...' and the need for a systematic risk assessment before proceeding with the project and such a large investment.

A series of chapters forefront the biological riches of Great Nicobar. The chapter by B. Chaudhuri describes how the islands' geographical and ecological isolation contributed to their unique diversity and endemism. Ishika Ramakrishna presents a nuanced account of the Nicobar long-tailed macaques and their interactions with people while criticising the infrastructure project EIA for misrepresenting and villainising the primate. Uday Mondal highlights the value of different habitats, from the pelagic to coastal mudflats and mangroves to rainforests, for the birds of Great Nicobar, including many endemics and migratory birds.

An evocative chapter by S. Harikrishnan on amphibians and reptiles sparkles with details of the many fascinating and endemic species from camouflaged forest lizards and giant geckos with blue-green eyes to the large Shompen frog, colourful cricket frogs and many others found on the island. The chapters by Mahi Mankeshwar and Shrishtee Bajpai highlight species of marine megafauna, including whales, dolphins, and leatherback sea turtles, found in the waters around the island. Like the visible tip of a submerged mountain, these lifeforms are a tantalising subset of the biological riches of Great Nicobar, where many new species undoubtedly await scientific discovery.

Benefits to a Few Might Be a Cost to Many

Two chapters, by social scientists Manish Chandi and Ajay Saini, touch upon the lives of the Indigenous and settler communities and their vulnerabilities, especially in relation to the forces of 'development' and the juggernaut of the project that seems set to further marginalise them. Even as the Nicobarese await returning to their original settlements from which they were earlier displaced by the tsunami, in what appears to be a bureaucratic sleight-of-hand, the authorities managed to obtain a letter of consent for the project from the Tribal Council. Subsequently, learning that they had been misinformed, the Tribal Council withdrew its consent for the project, as detailed in one of the Annexures to the book. As of today, their pleas remain unheard and unaddressed by the powers that be.

Together, the chapters in the book attest to how the remarkable crucible of nature that is Great Nicobar has thrived for ages alongside the Indigenous Shompen and Nicobarese people. It is a pity that instead of showcasing Great Nicobar as a sterling example of conservation and human–nature coexistence in a time of global climate crisis, the government is pursuing the giant port and infrastructure project that appears geared to leave this tapestry in tatters.

The last port of call for a concerned Indian citizen in the face of environmental negligence, destruction and injustice has been the judiciary, which, to its credit, has often stepped up to safeguard the environment. However, in the case of Great Nicobar, the events so far bring little credit to the judiciary as detailed in a chapter by journalist Aathira Perinchery and in another by advocate Norma Alvares. The latter presents an incisive analysis of the cases brought to the National Green Tribunal, the irregularities in its functioning, and the flawed judgements that have emerged to date. One hopes that more critical adjudication and better sense will prevail.

A Compilation and a Clarion Call

Overall, the book chapters, along with the useful tables, informative boxes, and annexures documenting the timeline and various petitions, largely achieve their purpose of drawing critical attention to an issue of enormous importance. The book could have gone further by presenting an overview chapter on Great Nicobar, including relevant maps, and also bringing additional perspectives to critically assess the strategic aspects of the project and the economic feasibility of the port.

As Vaishna Roy, editor of *Frontline* magazine where a number of the essays first appeared, writes in an opening note: 'While this strategic importance is undeniable, as is the need to bring about economic and material progress on the island, the colossal scale of the project is short-sighted and self-destructive. A small and self-contained scheme that does not threaten the ecology or the indigene population but works towards inclusive growth would have been more fitting.' This idea could have been fleshed out or given more attention in the book.

The Great Nicobar Betrayal appears at a crucial time to create public awareness and stimulate discussions on a project that deserves much closer and critical scrutiny. It also suggests a different response than that of Márquez's novella. In the novella, no one, despite being aware of the foretold death, is able to avert it. A reader may be left with little more to do than to savour the pleasure of a story well told or to ruminate on human fickleness and failings. But the voices of leading scientists, writers and nature's advocates in *The Great Nicobar Betrayal* do not just deliver grim prognoses to leave one with a sense of despair. This timely book alerts the government, the judiciary, and citizens to the need for a critical rethink on the project. It also serves as a clarion call to those concerned with nature and the nation to lend their support to those striving to stave off the disaster yet to unfold.

(First published in *Mongabay* India, 19 August 2024.)

Annexure 2

Letters Between Jairam Ramesh and Bhupender Yadav

Jairam Ramesh
Member of Parliament
(Rajya Sabha)

Dear Bhupendraji,

You may recall our recent exchange in the Rajya Sabha during Question Hour.

The Union Government's proposed Rs. 72,000 crore "Mega Infra Project" in Great Nicobar Island is a grave threat to Great Nicobar Island's tribal communities and natural ecosystem. The project can have catastrophic ecological and human consequences and has been pushed through by violating due process and sidestepping legal and Constitutional provisions protecting Tribal communities.

First, the project will require the diversion of 13,075 hectares of forest land - 15% of the island's area, and a nationally and globally unique rainforest ecosystem.

- Compensatory afforestation, which is no substitute whatsoever for the loss of natural biodiversity-rich forests, is being planned thousands of kilometres away and in a vastly different ecology.
- Parts of the project site reportedly come under CRZ 1A (areas with turtle nesting sites, mangroves, coral reefs), as had been noted in an National Green Tribunal (NGT) order in response to petitions challenging the clearances. Port construction is prohibited in this zone.
- However, recently, a High-Powered Committee (HPC) set up by the NGT has concluded that the port does not fall in CRZ-1A, but in CRZ-1B where port construction is allowed.

Residence Address: C1/9, Lodhi Garden, Rajesh Pilot Marg, New Delhi-110003, Phone: 011-24635888

- The HPC's conclusions are at variance with the information submitted by the Andaman and Nicobar Coastal Management Authority. The HPC's operations have been opaque – details of its ground-truthing activities and its report has not been made public, and the new information that would have justified the recategorization of the land has not been provided to stakeholders.

Second, the project can potentially result in the genocide of the Shompen, an indigenous community classified as a Particularly Vulnerable Tribal Group (PVTG). The project has been rammed through in violation of all legal and policy safeguards for the protection of tribal groups:

- The Tribal Council of the Islands was not adequately consulted, as is legally required. The Tribal Council of Great Nicobar Island has in fact expressed objections to the Project, claiming that the authorities had earlier "rushed them" into signing a "No Objection" letter based on misleading information – and that the No Objection letter has since been revoked
- The Island's Shompen Policy, notified by the Union Ministry of Tribal Affairs, which requires authorities to prioritise the tribe's welfare when considering "large scale development proposals" was neglected.
- Consultations with the Scheduled Tribes Commission, legally mandated by Article 338(9) of the Indian Constitution, appear to have been skipped
- The "Social Impact Assessment" conducted as part of the Right to Fair Compensation and Transparency in Land Acquisition, Rehabilitation and Resettlement Act, 2013 (RFCTLARR) ignored the existence of the Shompen and the Nicobarese
- The Project violates the letter and spirit of the Forest Rights Act (2006), which holds the Shompen as the sole legally empowered authority to protect, preserve, regulate and manage the tribal reserve

Third, the coastline where the port and the project is proposed to come up is an earthquake prone zone, and saw a permanent subsidence of about 15 feet during the tsunami of December 2004. Locating such a massive project here deliberately jeopardises investment, infrastructure, people, and the ecology.

Given these numerous violations of due processes, all clearances accorded to this short-sighted project must be suspended. The proposed project should be reviewed thoroughly and impartially, including by the Parliamentary committees concerned. The Ministry of Environment, Forests and Climate Change must fulfil its *dharma*—and not allow itself to be reduced to becoming a project proponent, especially when the project has decidedly disastrous human, social and ecological consequences.

With warm personal regards,

Jairam Ramesh
10/8/24

Shri Bhupender Yadav
Minister of Environment, Forests and Climate Change
New Delhi

मंत्री
पर्यावरण, वन एवं जलवायु परिवर्तन
भारत सरकार

MINISTER
ENVIRONMENT, FOREST AND CLIMATE CHANGE
GOVERNMENT OF INDIA

भूपेन्द्र यादव
BHUPENDER YADAV

D.O. No. IA3-2/12/2024.III   Date: 21st August, 2024

Dear Shri Jairam Ramesh ji,

Please refer to your letter dated 10th August, 2024 regarding the concerns raised by you on various aspects of "Holistic development of Great Nicobar Project" for which the Environment and Coastal Regulation Zone Clearance as well as the Forest Clearance was granted by the Ministry on 11.11.2022. I would like to draw your kind attention to factual status as mentioned in the Annexure in respect of each of the issues raised in your aforesaid letter.

The enclosed Annexure brings out the detailed and meticulous due diligence which has been observed in granting the aforesaid clearances while adhering to the provisions of the EIA Notifications, as amended and to the extant rules/regulations/guidelines.

I trust this addresses your concerns.

With regards,

Yours sincerely,

(Bhupender Yadav)

Shri Jairam Ramesh
Member of Parliament (Rajya Sabha)
C-I/9, Lodhi Garden,
Rajesh Pilot Marg,
New Delhi – 110003

Encl: As above.

Annexure

1. The Environment and Forest Clearances to the Project proposal having strategic, defence and national importance as well as involving development of Great Nicobar Island Project have been granted after due diligence and consideration of possible potential impacts on the ecology of the area and after ensuring that the legal safeguards and constitutional provisions related to the tribal communities have been duly followed.

2. The various aspects related to the project viz. high biodiversity, economic importance, coral colonies, aboriginal tribes, wildlife issues, etc. have been diligently considered by the Central Government. It is only after due deliberations and after incorporating exemplary mitigation measures that the decision on the project was taken by the Central Government keeping the strategic, national and defence interests in mind and without compromising with the environmental and social aspects. For this, detailed Environmental Impact Assessment (EIA) studies were carried out and an Environmental Management Plan (EMP) has been prepared which, inter alia, includes mitigation measures to minimize the impact during construction and operation phases of the project. The Environmental Clearance accorded comprises as many as 42 specific conditions dealing with each component of the project, in addition to all standard conditions applicable to each component dealing with statutory compliances, air quality monitoring and preservation, water quality monitoring and preservation, noise monitoring and preservation, energy conservation measures, waste management, green belt, marine ecology, transport, human health environment and risk mitigation and disaster management.

3. It is only after examining the conservation measures envisaged for safeguarding the critical ecosystems and allied taxa that the Central Government has considered the project for approval under the Van (Sanrakshan Evam Samvardhan) Adhiniyam, 1980. The recommendations of Prof. Shekhar Singh and the order of Hon'ble Supreme Court dated 7th May 2002 shall be complied during the implementation of the project.

4. It is because of the rigor of environmental scrutiny and after incorporating the consequent safeguards that the Environment and Forest Clearances were granted. The Environmental and Forest Clearances so granted has withstood judicial scrutiny . Reference may be made of the Hon'ble NGTs order dated 3rd April, 2023 wherein Hon'ble NGT in the last sentence of para 32 of the order referred to above stated that "Thus, by and large the project is compliant and EC does not call for interference." At para 29 of the same order of NGT has also mentioned that "Considering the above, we do not find any ground to interfere with the FC".

5. Responding to the specific concerns, it is stated that the diversion of forest for the instant project is as per the provisions of the National Forest Policy, 1988, which states that in hills and in mountain regions, the aim should be to maintain two-third of the area under forest cover. Despite the diversion of proposed forest land for this project in Great Nicobar Island, 82% of the area of Great Nicobar continues to be under Protected Forests, National Parks, Eco Sensitive Zones and Biosphere Reserve for the conservation of biodiversity at ecosystem, species and

genetic levels. This is much more than the laid down norms of maintaining two thirds of the area under forest cover in hilly and mountainous areas while implementing development projects as mentioned above.

6. The project would be implemented in a phased manner, in three phases, in a period of almost 30 years. Moreover, a major portion of the proposed area is earmarked for green development where no tree felling is envisaged. The potential felling of trees will be less than the half of the total trees enumerated/estimated and felling will be undertaken in phased manner. Further, it is also expected that about 15% of development area will remain as green and open spaces.

7. Since the areas for plantation are not available in the Great Nicobar Island, the plantation of native species in the non-notified forest lands in the arid landscape and in the vicinity of the urban areas would provide greater ecological value. Accordingly Compensatory Afforestation (CA) is proposed to be carried out in the States of Haryana (including Aravallis), Madhya Pradesh or in States adjoining to NCR, over non-notified forest land/degraded land, double in extent to the area being diverted. The non- notified forest land taken up for CA will be notified as Reserve Forest/Protected Forest. This will not only improve the flow of ecosystem goods and services but also add to the total notified forest area of the country. Already an area of 24353.72 Ha has been notified as Protected Forest by Haryana Government.

8. Another issue raised in your letter is that the HPC's operation have been opaque and that its report has not been made public and that its conclusions are at variance with the information submitted by the Andaman and Nicobar Coastal management Authority. It has also been mentioned that the NGT order mentioned that parts of the Project came under CRZ-1A . In fact, to the contrary, Hon'ble NGT did not made any such categorical statement but, instead, NGT directed the constitution of High-Powered Committee (HPC) to examine, among other issues , the issue as to whether any part of the Project site fell under CRZ-IA .

9. As directed by NGT, the HPC, under the Chairmanship of the Secretary, EF&CC and comprising other members namely Chief Secretary, Andaman & Nicobar, Zoological Survey of India, Botanical Survey of India, Central Pollution Control Board, nominee of Vice Chairman of Niti Aayog. nominee of Secretary, Ministry of Shipping and Director, Wildlife Institute of India convened three meetings on 18.04.2023, 02.05.2023 and 04.07.2023.

10. On the directions of HPC the concerned Agency, i.e., the National Centre for Sustainable Costal Management (NCSCM) visited the project site and its nearby areas and undertook extensive ground truthing to determine status of High Tide Line, Low Tide Line and Ecologically Sensitive Areas (ESA) for the proposed Port Area/ International Container Transhipment Terminal (ICTT) at Galathea Bay in Great Nicobar Island. Thereafter, taking into consideration the factual position, layout of the project prepared by the Andaman & Nicobar Islands Integrated Development Corporation Limited (ANIIDCO), observations made during the ground truthing exercise and in terms of the response received by the Forest Department of UT Administration and Project Proponent, the NCSCM concluded that no portion of the proposed port falls in CRZ-IA. Apart from this, the Project Proponent ANIIDCO is also bound by the specific condition IX of the EC, which prohibits construction works in the Coastal Regulation Zone area, other than those permitted in the

Coastal Regulation Zone Notification . Specific Condition IX of the Environmental Clearance states that *"Construction activity shall be carried out strictly according to the provisions of the ICRZ Notification, 2019. No construction works other than those permitted in Coastal Regulation Zone Notification shall be carried out in the Coastal Regulation Zone area".* Further, in compliance with ICRZ Notification, development within CRZ area will be in compliance with ICRZ Notification 2019 and no construction works other than those permitted in Coastal Regulation Zone Notification shall be carried out in Coastal Regulation Zone area. It is re-iterated that that no activity is proposed to be undertaken by ANIIDCO within ICRZ-IA (Turtle nesting/Megapode nesting/ Biosphere reserve).

11. As regards , the observation that the operations of HPC are opaque , it is clarified that the Project is of national importance with strategic and defence dimensions. These aspects of the project were also taken note of by the HPC while examining the observations of the NGT in its report on the issues referred to it by Hon'ble NGT. It is against this background that the record of HPC deliberations have not been shared with the public.

12. The importance of the Project from defence, strategic and national importance can be gauged from the fact that the Hon'ble NGT which is charged with the responsibility of effective and expeditious disposal of cases relating to environmental protection and conservation of forests and other natural resources including enforcement of any legal right relating to environment and giving relief and compensation for damages to persons and property and for matters connected therewith or incidental thereto has on its own in para 26 of the aforesaid order observed that : "From above resume, it is patent that the project has great significance not only for economic development of the island and surrounding areas of strategic location but also for defence and national security. Even the appellants have not joined issue on these aspects. While the Tribunal's consideration is confined to material on record, we have also noted (without any comment) media reports that the area is located in China's 'string of pearls' strategy1 which is sought to be countered by Indian Authorities under India's 'Act East' policy. Indian Ocean has emerged as a key intersection zone of Indian and Chinese strategic interests. There are further media reports of huge poaching of environmental marine resources of Andaman by poachers from Myanmar for which number of people have been arrested. Poaching activities include destruction of corals, killing of sharks, taking away of valuable fishes. The project will help bridge infrastructural gap in island and promote international trade saving huge amount on transhipment cargo."

13. Against the aforesaid observations of NGT itself, importance of the Project from national, defence and strategic importance cannot be overemphasised. Accordingly, it would be incorrect to state that the proposed 'Mega Infra Project" was a grave threat to Great Nicobar Island's tribal communities and natural ecosystem.

14. As regards concerns regarding the allegation related to violation of policy and legal safeguards of the tribal community and issues related thereto are concerned, it is worth mentioning that all procedures mandated in the Act/Regulations/ Policies have been followed. Further, due consultation with the tribal experts including AnSI (Anthropological Survey of India)has also been done in order to ensure the safety,

protection, welfare and wellbeing of the PVTGs in the wake of Holistic Development of GNI project. The Empowered Committee in its observations has clearly stated that the interests of tribal population especially Shompen, a Particularly Vulnerable Tribal Group will not be affected adversely and that the displacement of tribals would not be allowed. A & N Administration has also made adequate budget provisions for tribal welfare plans throughout the Project period and beyond in compliance of EC & CRZ Clearances. The only habitation of Shompens or Nicobarese in the project area is at New Chingen, Rajiv Nagar and the Administration is not proposing displacement of any tribal habitations. Further, due consultation with the tribal experts including Anthropological Survey of India (AnSI) was also conducted.

15. The President of India has delegated the powers of the State Government to the Administrator/Hon'ble Lt. Governor, A & N Islands under the Scheduled Tribes and Other Traditional Forests Dwellers (Recognition of Forests Rights) Act, 2006 within the Union Territory. Accordingly, Sub-Divisional Level Committee (SDLC) and District level Committee (DLC) have been constituted. Further, the field functionaries of Andaman Adim Janjati Vikas Samiti (AAJVS) which is working for the welfare of PVTGs since 1976 onwards have been included in the Sub Divisional Committee and District Level Committee constituted under Forest Rights Act to represent the Shompen tribe to provide valuable insights into the concerns of tribal communities and work closely with the tribal communities, understand their needs and challenges, and help to design and implement programs that address their specific issues. With regard to Nicobari tribe, the office bearer of Tribal Council of Great Nicobar has been included as one of the members of FRA(Forest Rights Act) Committees. Consequently, RoFR (Recognition of Forest Rights) certificate has been issued on 18.08.2022 by the District level Committee (DLC) as per the FRA, 2006. As per section 6 (6) of FRA Act the decision of the District Level Committee on the record of the Forest Right is final and binding.

16. Public Consultation, which is an essential component of the steps laid down in the EIA Notification, 2006, was duly conducted for the Project . The Tribal communities of the region were duly represented at the public hearing through the Andaman Adim Janjati Vikas Samiti(AAJVS) whose views were also considered in order to ensure the safety, protection, welfare and wellbeing of the Particularly Vulnerable Tribal Groups (PVTGs) in the wake of Holistic Development of GNI project. The Chairman, Tribal Council (Great Nicobar & Little Nicobar Island) also attended the public hearing held in connection with Environmental Clearance and EIA for the GNI project, on behalf of the tribal community and no objections were raised. It may be mentioned that the District Level Committee of Nicobar District has approved the record of forest rights prepared by the Sub-Division Level Committee (SLDC), headed by Assistant Commissioner in the meeting held on 18.08.2022. The Chairman of the Tribal Council, Campbell Bay, Little and Great Nicobar were duly consulted and no objections were raised during the statutory period prescribed in the Scheduled Tribes and Other Traditional Forest Dwellers (Recognition of Forest Rights) Act, 2006.

17. The Administration is following the objectives of the Shompen policy to ensure their integrity and wellbeing through developing channels of communication, consultation and participation only based on their willingness. A & N Administration has prepared budget of Rs. 201.98 crores for tribal welfare plans including setting

up of special medical unit to be implemented for a period of 50 years in compliance with EC & CRZ Clearance.

18. In lieu of 73.07 sq.Kms. being required for the purposes of the Project, 76.98 Sq.Kms. is being re-notified as tribal reserve resulting in a net addition of 3.912 sq. kms area in tribal reserve area of Great Nicobar Island. Section 3 of A&N (Protection of Aboriginal Tribes) Regulation, 1956 empowers A&N Administration to declare reserve Tribal area specifying the limits of such area.

19. The Empowered Committee of UT Administration recommended de-notification of Tribal Reserve and Ministry of Tribal Affairs conveyed its no objection for the proposal for de-notification of tribal reserve area in Great Nicobar Island subject to compliance under Scheduled Tribes and other Traditional Forest Dwellers (Recognition of Forest Rights) Act, 2006. The Empowered Committee, constituted by the Hon'ble Lt. Governor, Andaman and Nicobar Administration, including the Head of Office/Superintending Anthropologist, AnSI, Port Blair, and anthropologists such as Prof. Visvajit Pandya as members discussed the issue related to the impact of the Project at length to ensure that the interests of the tribes of Great Nicobar Island are duly protected during the holistic development of the GNI project. Further, the Empowered Committee deliberated the issue of impact of project on the tribes of GNI and it was unanimously observed that the de-notification of tribal reserved area be considered subject to the condition that the interests of tribal population especially Shompen, a Particularly Vulnerable Tribal Group (PVTG) are not affected adversely; there is strict implementation of the provisions of Protection of Aboriginal Tribes (PAT) Regulation to protect the interest of the Shompen and that the displacement of tribals is not permitted.

20. The development plan is in sync with the Shompen Policy and in fact, the Policy allows large scale development proposals in Great Nicobar Island subject to consultation with the Ministry, Directorate of Tribal Welfare and AAJVS. The necessary consultation with the Ministry of Tribal Affairs, Govt. of India was also carried out and it is based on the recommendation of Empowered Committee that No Objection Certificate was also issued by the Ministry. It is pertinent to mention that the project will not disturb or displace any Shompens.

21. Another issue which has been raised is that Social Impact Assessment has not been carried out as per the provisions of Right to Fair Compensation & Transparency in Land Acquisition, Rehabilitation & Resettlement Act, 2013. This is not factually correct. Bare minimum acquisition of land from private land owners has been proposed for critical infrastructure including international airport, roads, etc. as part of holistic development of Great Nicobar Island project. Social Welfare Department, A & N Administration has appointed M/s Probe Research & Social Development Pvt. Ltd. for Social Impact Assessment (SIA) study for acquisition of private land for airport. As per the report submitted by the agency, the total private land to be acquired for the airport project is 404.82 hectares. There are 263 families who are getting directly affected because of the land acquisition for construction of the airport. The said SIA study focuses on the families who will have to part with their land for the Airport development project.

22. As part of the aforesaid SIA study, public hearing was held on 28.06.2024 at Gandhinagar Community Hall, Campbell Bay for submitting comments & objections

of all the stakeholders. The final report of the assessment has been submitted to the Social Welfare Department for further review. Additionally, as per the Right to Fair Compensation & Transparency in Land Acquisition, Rehabilitation & Resettlement Act, 2013 an expert group has been constituted vide order dated 30.07.2024 with the approval of Hon'ble Lt. Governor to evaluate the report and provide recommendations, the report of which is awaited. This group includes two external social experts along with other committee members to ensure a comprehensive and unbiased review. Further, the project proponent has also given an undertaking that the R&R for the affected families will be provided as per the Right to Fair Compensation and Transparency in Land Acquisition, Rehabilitation and Resettlement Act, 2013.

23. Specific Conditions of the Environment Clearance make it incumbent on the Project Proponent to provide compensation as per the extant legal and administrative framework including as per the provisions of Right to Fair Compensation and Transparency in Land Acquisition, Rehabilitation and Resettlement Act, 2013.

24. As regards the issue of non-compliance with the provisions of Article338(9) of the Constitution, Article 338(9) of the Indian Constitution dealing with National Commission for Scheduled Castes provides that "The Union and every State Government shall consult the Commission on all major policy matters affecting Scheduled Castes". Similar provision in respect of National Commission for Scheduled Tribe is provided for under Article 338A(9) which states that "The Union and every State Government shall consult the Commission on all major policy matters affecting Scheduled Tribes". It would be relevant to mention here that the UT of A&N has not undertaken any new Policy measure affecting the Scheduled Tribe except that a development Project is being implemented in Great Nicobar. The development plan is in sync with the Shompen Policy and in fact, the Policy allows large scale development proposals in Great Nicobar Island subject to consultation with the Ministry, Directorate of Tribal Welfare and AAJVS. The necessary consultation with the Ministry of Tribal Affairs, Govt. of India was also carried out and it is based on the recommendation of Empowered Committee, No Objection Certificate was also issued by the Ministry.

25. Another concern raised by you is regarding the Project being located in coastline which is an earthquake prone zone. Seismologists suggest a Return Period of 420–750 years for mega-earthquakes similar to that which occurred in 2004. In the next 5–10 year period, the ANI area can generate an earthquake with a magnitude of around 5.5 to 6.4 Mw. The medium strength earthquake of 6.4 to 6.7 Mw is possible in next 30 years. The strong earthquake of 6.7 to 7 Mw is possible in next 50 years. However, the probability of a mega earthquake of 9.2 that happened in 2004 is low. The risk assessment study has been carried out based on the two source – anthropogenic and natural disasters and its vulnerability and disaster management plan have been prepared accordingly. In the EIA document the detailed risk assessment study has been carried out. It would be pertinent to mention here that the Indian Standard Code of Practice for Earthquake Resistant Design and Construction of Buildings (IS 13827), Bureau of Indian Standards (IS 1893, 2002) and Indian Standard Criteria for Earthquake Resistant Design of Structures (IS 4326, 1993) along with NBC guidelines shall be followed while designing the various building structures as part of the Holistic development of GNI.

Jairam Ramesh
Member of Parliament
(Rajya Sabha)

Dear Bhupender-ji:

First of all, many thanks for your detailed response of August 21, 2024 to my letter of August 10, 2024, on the proposed Great Nicobar infra project. I have studied your reply carefully and have the following detailed comments to offer.

1. The Ministry notes that the project has been approved after a Environmental Impact Assessment (EIA) study. Yet, an examination of the EIA raises various red flags. For instance, Chapter 5 of the EIA report which describes the alternate sites considered for the project has omitted the least environmentally destructive site, Campbell Bay, and only included the other 3 sites which are either as or marginally more environmentally sensitive than Galathea Bay. This was pointed out by the Expert Appraisal Committee (EAC) in its 260th meeting during 5th-6th April, 2021. Point No. 4 reads: "The Committee notes that the site selection for the port component has been done keeping primarily the technical and financial viability in place. The environmental aspects were not given much weightage while selecting the site." Moreover, given that the Galathea Wildlife Sanctuary was de-notified in January 2021 for the purpose of making the port and that the proposal for diverting about 130 sq km of forest area was sent in October 2020 (that is before the EIA consultant did an analyses of the alternative sites), any analyses conducted would be unlikely to deviate from the already fixed location of the projects by NITI Aayog. The **EIA therefore appears to have been primed to ensure clearance of the project in the form proposed by the NITI Aayog.**

2. The Ministry also defends the projects by citing the preparation of an Environmental Management Plan (EMP). However, it must be noted that the Final EIA report that was submitted to the EAC-Infra I committee was devoid of any sound mitigation measures or a robust EMP. It was **only** after the committee's comments that the mitigation measures were prepared. These reports include unscientific and untested mitigation measures, with the conservation and management plan relying largely on translocation, which is successful only in hardy and generalist species. The plan to translocate coral reefs is also entirely impractical, since they are an exceptionally complex and diverse ecosystem constituting all the trophic levels analogous to a rainforest. Ecosystems cannot be shifted artificially. The reports are also insufficient in their scope, with the WII's report on the conservation and long-term monitoring of sea turtles being entirely silent on the impact of the dredging, piling, land reclamation, and other construction activities for the port and the airport that will affect not only the nesting but feeding and foraging grounds of sea turtles. Moreover, by the WII's own admission, it has not conducted any studies on the Giant leatherback turtles or any other species of sea turtles in the Andaman and Nicobar Islands. **Various dimensions of the EMP therefore appear to be hastily drawn up, and unscientific and impractical in their scope.**

3. The Ministry notes that the Environmental Clearance (EC) accorded to the project comprises 42 specific conditions dealing with each aspect of the project. So far, the **implementation of these conditions does not inspire much confidence.** For instance, the detailed plans for long term monitoring and management that have been prepared by the WII, SACON, Zoological Survey of India (ZSI), and Botanical Survey of India (BSI) have not been made public yet. This is a failure to meet Condition VI of the 'Other Specific Conditions' section of the Environmental Clearance, which mandated that these reports be put up on the websites of the Andaman and Nicobar Forest Department.

4. The Ministry claims that the project will comply with the recommendations of the commission headed by Prof. Shekhar Singh. The very first recommendation made by the Shekhar Singh Commission is that the "**Felling of trees** and collection of non-timber forest produce should be **banned** from the forests of Little Andaman

Island and **all tribal reserves**..." The third recommendation states that "In addition to areas covered under 1 and 2 above, **no felling of trees should be allowed in any unworked forest area**, i.e., area where felling of trees as per working plans, working schemes, felling schemes, or approved working plans has not taken place earlier. There should also be no diversion of forestland from any such unworked area...without the specific orders of the Supreme Court." It is evident that the planned diversion of forests on Great Nicobar Island actually stands in violation of the recommendations, especially since the area includes a tribal reserve which is being denotified.

5. The Ministry has argued that the Environmental and Forest Clearances granted have withstood judicial scrutiny by the National Green Tribunal. However, this is an incomplete truth - the NGT order did find a need to formulate a High-Powered Committee (HPC) to evaluate the Environmental and CRZ Clearances granted to the project and placed a temporary stay on any irreversible activities pertaining to the project. The judgment indicates that the HPC's mandate was to re-examine the entire Environmental Clearance. Point number 33 of the NGT's order states that "[T]here are some **unanswered deficiencies** pointed out by the appellants which need to be addressed...These aspects may call for revisiting the EC by a High-Powered Committee (HPC) which we propose to constitute." **The NGT order therefore is not the clean chit for the project** that the Ministry has made it out to be.

6. The Ministry says that the National Forest Policy, 1988, requires two-thirds of the land area in hill and mountain regions to be forested, and that even after the diversion for this project, 82% of the land area on Great Nicobar will continue to be forested. The National Forest Policy, however, specifically states that "Tropical rain/moist forests, particularly in areas like Arunachal Pradesh, Kerala, Andaman & Nicobar Islands, should be **totally safeguarded**." The **application of the 2/3rd standard for hills and mountain regions is deceptive**. The standard that the Ministry should uphold is that forest cover on Andaman and Nicobar should be 'totally safeguarded.' Moreover, the forests of Great Nicobar Island are not homogenous - the composition of coastal forests is different from inland forests, and both support unique biodiversity. The figure of 82% of land area being protected is therefore illusory and obscures details

of which forests will be more impacted. Finally, in the master plan report submitted by AECOM (*a real estate development firm tasked by the NITI Aayog to draft a pre-feasibility report for the holistic development of Great Nicobar in 2021*), the original plan for the project also involves a large part of the West Coast where ancillary facilities are to be developed in the second phase. This will likely involve another major diversion of forested land.

7. The Ministry has noted that "the potential felling of trees will be less than half of the total trees enumerated…15% of development area will remain as green and open spaces." However, this argument is premised on a faulty understanding of ecosystem functioning. The key consideration for policymakers should be the **preservation of the composite forest ecosystem**, given its ecological value and biodiversity. Any desecration and fragmentation of these old-growth natural forest ecosystem will be a travesty that will detract from our national and international sustainability efforts and endanger the island's endemic flora and fauna, even if individual trees remain. Furthermore, even if only half of the enumerated trees are felled, it would still mean the **cutting of half a million trees** – a travesty by any standard. Finally, this also raises questions on the environmental due diligence done on the project. If a major portion of the area is earmarked for green development and only half the trees estimated to be felled will be felled, why is the entire area being diverted? Why is an exact estimation of tree felling still not available, and why is the method of tree enumeration not mentioned in the EIA report?

8. One of the key objections to the Great Nicobar Mega Infra Project is that the **compensatory afforestation – never a substitute for the loss of biodiversity-rich natural forest ecosystems** – is being conducted in the distant states of Haryana, Madhya Pradesh, and other states adjoining the National Capital Region. The Ministry has justified this move on the grounds that areas for plantation are not available on Great Nicobar Island. The proposed solution, while certainly inventive, is focused on meeting the bureaucratic requirements of the law, rather than upholding its spirit. The lack of availability of land in a similar biome speaks to the distinctive and unique ecosystem and geography of Great Nicobar Island.

9. The Ministry denies that the National Green Tribunal (NGT) ever classified parts of the project as being in ICRZ-IA. This appears to be untrue. The table on Point 24 of the order clearly shows **7.07 sq km as being in ICRZ IA zone,** including 0.67 sq km of the proposed port. Point 33 further reiterates it, noting that "it is also shown that **part of the project is in CRZ IA area** where Port is prohibited. These aspects may call for revisiting the EC by a High-Powered Committee (HPC) which we propose to constitute." Thus, contrary to the Minister's claim, the **NGT explicitly acknowledged that the project, including the port, was proposed on land classified as ICRZ-IA,** and formed an HPC to investigate it.

10. The Ministry gives details of the ground-truthing exercise conducted by the National Centre for Sustainable Costal Management (NCSCM) on the directions of the HPC and cites its findings to claim that no portion of the proposed port falls in ICRZ-IA. However, the HPC 's original mandate, as per the NGT order cited previously, was to revisit the Environment Clearance given that the project falls in areas protected under ICRZ-IA. The HPC has been inventive by actually revisiting and modifying the nature of the categorisation from 1A to 1B. The **NCSM's findings are also at odds with all available evidence.** For instance, as per the Environmental Clearance, there are 51 Megapode nests and 20668 coral colonies located in the site of the project. The importance of Galathea as a turtle nesting beach is also well known and is pointed out in the National Marine Turtle Plan published in 2021. By definition, any areas that have corals, turtle nesting sites and ground nesting birds are categorized as ICRZ-1A area. The HPC's reclassification of land from ICRZ IA to IB is very hard to believe – especially since the findings of the ground truthing exercise have not been made public.

11. The Ministry has noted that the project is of national importance with strategic and defence dimensions and that it is against this background that the record of HPC deliberations have not been shared with the public. **The project is largely commercial,** with only 12.6 sq km of township being defence related, and the airport being military-cum-civilian use. The mandate of the HPC was to revisit the Environmental and CRZ Clearances, most documents relating to which are already available in the public domain. The specific project under consideration is the 100% commercial transshipment port, and

the issue specifically being discussed is the legal categorisation of coastal land. There is no reason as to why the deliberations of the HPC regarding the entire project area needs to remain confidential. **Information in the public interest on a commercial project should not be denied using the cover of national security** – it sets a very poor precedent for transparency. This opacity also raises suspicion on the intent and the methods employed by the HPC, which has been tasked scrutinizing the clearances but comprises members of the very same agencies who facilitated the clearance.

12. The Ministry stresses that the "[I]mportance of the Project from national defence and strategic importance cannot be overemphasized. Accordingly, it would be incorrect to state that the proposed 'Mega Infra Project' was a grave threat to Great Nicobar Island's tribal communities and natural ecosystem." This is a patently absurd and extremely dangerous line of thinking. Even if one were to accept the strategic and defence importance of the Project, it would not preclude any discussion of its impact on the island's tribal communities and natural ecosystem. **Nobody can be against "strategic considerations" but surely a better balance between them and ecological concerns can and must be struck which is certainly missing in this case.**

13. With regards to the Shompen community, the Ministry notes that "the only habitation of Shompens or Nicobarese in the project area is at New Chingen, Rajiv Nagar and the Administration is not proposing displacement of any tribal habitations." However, the Shompen are a Particularly Vulnerable Tribal Group (PVTG), and direct displacement of the community is not the only threat to its existence. The project will require a **large-scale influx of people and tourists,** and the Shompen tribe may be ill-equipped to navigate this social contact. The population expansion will also inevitably **generate ecological and resource pressures on the land, forest, and water resources of the island,** directly affecting the Shompen and the Nicobarese tribals. The Shompen Policy (2015) specifically pays attention to the "integrity" of the community, which is under threat from this project. Additionally, the development of the project will de jure displace the Great Nicobarese, whose ancestral villages – which they evacuated after the tsunami of 2004 – fall in the project's proposed land area. **The project will foreclose any**

possibility of the community's aspiration of returning to its ancestral villages and is therefore a permanent displacement for the Nicobarese tribals.

14. The Ministry argues that the public consultation for the project was duly conducted, that the island's tribal communities were represented at the public hearing through the Andaman Adim Janjati Vikas Samiti (AAJVS) and the Chairman, Tribal Council (Great Nicobar &Little Nicobar Island), and that "no objections were raised." However, it fails to mention that the **Chairman had very clearly said that they wish to return to their ancestral villages** – the project will preclude such a possibility. This aspiration of the community raised by the Tribal Council Chairman was entirely ignored and not addressed at any point in the process of the Environmental Clearance. Nor was there any consideration given to the letter submitted by the members of the Indian Anthropological Association during the Public Hearing which listed out the impact of the project on the indigenous communities of the island. The Tribal Council of Great Nicobar Island has since expressed objections to the Project, claiming that the authorities had earlier "rushed them" into signing a "No objection" letter based on misleading information. **The Tribal Council has also revoked the No Objection letter.** The communities impacted by the project – the Shompen and the Nicobarese - are extremely marginalized and have been excluded from the policymaking apparatus of the Andaman and Nicobar Islands, historically and up until the present day. Given the long history of social exclusion, and the dynamics of exploitation involved therein, ignoring the legitimate grievances of the tribal groups is deeply unjust. **Hyper-technical and hyper-bureaucratic approaches are inappropriate in this context.**

15. The Ministry notes that the Sub-Division Level Committee (SDLC) constituted to oversee the Forest Rights Act has issued the Recognition of Forest Rights certificate and that it has been approved by the District Level Committee, making the project compliant with the FRA. Furthermore, it claims that "no objections were raised during the statutory period prescribed" by the Chairman of the Tribal Council and the officers of the Andaman Adim Janjati Vikas Samiti (AAJVS). However, during the meetings held among the SDLC members between the 13th – 16th of August, 2022, the officer of AAJVS had

clearly mentioned that the Shompen group in the Kokeon area will suffer because of the construction activities. **This statement was not recorded in the proceedings of the meeting of the SDLC, which came to light later in the letter dated 22nd, November 2022 in which the Tribal Council withdrew its consent for the diversion of the forest.**

16. The Ministry acknowledges that land is being denotified from the tribal reserve for the project, but attempts to minimise the issue by pointing to the additional land that is being renotified, which will result in a net addition of 3.912 sq kms. The tribal reserve is home to the Shompen, who are a Particularly Vulnerable Tribal Group (PVTG). The natural and social ecosystem has been their home for millennia, and large-scale, arbitrary changes to the tribal reserve boundaries – even if they result, on net, in a larger geographic area – leave the community ill-equipped to adapt to the new reality. The Shompen will seek – and rightly so – continued access to land and resources that has been in their community for generations, irrespective of the boundaries drawn on the official map. This denotification of tribal reserve land therefore threatens their social and economic existence. The Shompen Policy explicitly calls for **priority to be given to the "integrity" of the community,** precisely for such an eventuality.

17. The Ministry notes that the Empowered Committee of the UT Administration recommended de- notification of Tribal Reserve, and that the committee comprised anthropologists such as Prof. Visvajit Pandya. **Incidentally, the video report submitted by Prof. Pandya and his team shows the members of the Shompen community clearly stating that they are against any disturbances to their forested and riparian habitats, and members of the Great Nicobarese community reiterating their demand to return to their ancestral villages.** However, these submissions were not entered into the records and discussed by the committee. What was the purpose of the consultation by Prof. Pandya? Why were his comments, and the opinions of the Shompen and Great Nicobarese tribes, not considered by the committee? Was this merely a window-dressing exercise?

18. The Ministry claims that the development plan is "in sync" with the Shompen policy, since the Policy allows large scale development proposals in Great Nicobar Island. A cursory reading of the Shompen policy will reveal that it explicitly calls for "the welfare and integrity of the Shompen community" to be "given priority" in large-scale development proposals. It is evident that while some formal procedures have been undertaken to signify consideration of the community's interest, **priority has not been accorded to the community's needs**.

19. The Ministry claims that the Union Territory has not undertaken any new policy measure affecting the Scheduled Tribes, except that a development project is being implemented in Great Nicobar. It must be noted that the development project in question is not small. As its title itself signifies, it is a "mega project" that aims for a large-scale reshaping of the island's ecological, geological, and sociological structures and involves one of the largest single diversions of forest in India. It is **tantamount to a policy shift in its scale and consequence**. The Ministry's argument is based on technicality, rather than on a truthful account of the project's real-world impact. The authorities must consult the National Commission on Scheduled Tribes

20. The Ministry gives details of the project's Social Impact Assessment, which considered its impact on the 263 families directly affected by land acquisition for the construction of the airport. However, as argued in my letter of August 10, 2024, the Social Impact Assessment (SIA) for land acquisition must, *by law,* not concern only those affected by land acquisition directly, but all social stakeholders of the project in question. The **SIA, therefore, should have considered the impacts of the project on the larger community, including the Shompen and the Nicobarese tribals**. Additionally, the SIA does not consider the impact of the greater population and tourist burden on the island's water resources, rendering it insufficient for the defined purpose.

21. The Ministry has given an assurance that the rehabilitation of the affected families will occur as per the Land Acquisition Act of 2013. While this is legally required to be the case, it is disconcerting that even after the final SIA report has been published, **the residents have not been told where they are going to be relocated.** This is a community composed mostly of the families of ex-servicemen, who have been displaced twice (once settled from mainland and second time due to the tsunami). More sensitivity should have been shown to the families in this process of resettlement.

22. The last argument given by the Ministry points to a study that claims that a mega-earthquake of the scale which occurred in 2004 is likely to occur only after 420-750 years. The same 2019 study has been cited by the Environmental Impact Assessment (EIA) report to downplay the seismic risks on Great Nicobar Island. However, the aforementioned study uses a methodology highly limited in its scope and appears to focus on *tsunami risk* alone. The EIA also conveniently ignores other studies that independently conclude that the region of Great Nicobar and Sumatra is extremely likely (90% likelihood) to experience high magnitude (>7-8Mw) earthquake within 20-25 years. **Great Nicobar lies in one of the world's most earthquake prone regions, and given strength and location, these earthquakes can irreparably damage these infra projects.**

I hope the comments I have offered will be seen by you as a constructive contribution to the debate on a project which has far-reaching environmental and humanitarian consequences.

With warm personal regards,

Jairam Ramesh

27/8/24

Shri Bhupender Yadav
Minister of Environment, Forests and Climate Change
New Delhi

Jairam Ramesh
Member of Parliament
(Rajya Sabha)

Dear Bhupenderji:

I read news reports about the counter-affidavit filed by the Ministry of Environment, Forests and Climate Change in the National Green Tribunal on the Great Nicobar Island Development Project on which we have had detailed exchanges earlier.

First, I am shocked that the High-Powered Committee (HPC) constituted by the MoEF&CC in pursuance of the NGT's directive to review environmental and CRZ clearances did **NOT** associate any independent institution or expert when the NGT had given it the flexibility to do so. It is truly amazing that the HPC has among its members (i) NITI Aayog that conceived the project; (ii) the project proponent Andaman and Nicobar Islands Integrated Development Corporation (ANIIDCO);(iii) a representative of the MOEF&CC's Expert Appraisal Committee that recommended the clearances in the first place; and (iv) MOEF&CC that granted the clearances. Need I say anything more on the credibility and integrity of the HPC?

Second, the MOEF&CC had clearly diluted the NGT's directive and gave very limited terms of reference to the HPC. As I recall, the NGT gave only "by way of instance" just three "unanswered deficiencies". The terms of reference have been restricted to just these three examples cited by the NGT in its order that led to the constitution of the HPC. The HPC, howsoever biased by its very composition, has NOT carried out any meaningful and comprehensive reassessment as it had been directed to do.

Third, the HPC's report has been kept secret. I don't understand this: when the original process for grant of clearances itself was not classified as "privileged and confidential", how can a review, howsoever flawed, and that too mandated by the court be classified thus? How can a township focusing on promotion of tourism, a commercial trans-shipment port and a power plant be suddenly declared as "strategic projects" on which no public debate can take place?

Residence Address: C1/9, Lodhi Garden, Rajesh Pilot Marg, New Delhi-110003, Phone: 011-24635888

Fourth, as you well know, the categorization of coastal areas into zones is based on their ecological sensitivity. Construction activities are prohibited in certain zones. According to the NGT's order of April 2023, slightly over 7 square kms of the total project area fell in such a *prohibited* zone. Now, the MoEF&CC's counter-affidavit denies that this is the case. What is the basis of the dramatic U-turn and what confidence can be placed in the new set of facts being presented?

It is also a matter of grave concern that while the NGT deliberates on petitions before it, ANIIDCO has already invited expressions of interest that is a precursor for the clearing of around 65 square kms of biodiversity-rich forests. I believe the Government of India is hell-bent on inflicting an ecological and humanitarian disaster on our country.

With warm personal regards,

Jairam Ramesh
28/9/24

Shri Bhupender Yadav
Minister of Environment, Forests and Climate Change
New Delhi

ANNEXURE 3

Press Release by Association of Indian Primatologists (AIP)

17 March 2025

Press Release

This press release is in response to a media article reporting the disbursement of funds for the preparation of Wildlife Conservation Plans (WCPs) for several species including the Nicobar long-tailed macaque as part of the mega-scale construction project at Great Nicobar Island. As per a condition in the Environmental Clearance accorded to the project on 11 November 2022, a plan was to be prepared for the conservation of macaques till 2052, coinciding with the completion of the project and submitted within fifteen days from the grant of the clearance. This task was allotted to the Salim Ali Centre for Ornithology and Natural History (SACON), currently, the Wildlife Institute of

India's South India Centre. The compliance report submitted by the project proponent, Andaman and Nicobar Islands Integrated Development Corporation Limited (ANIIDCO) to the Ministry of Environment, Forests and Climate Change (MoEFCC), states that a conservation and management plan has been prepared by SACON for the Nicobar long-tailed macaque, robber crab and other endemic species for a period of thirty years and a cumulative allocation of Rs 230.77 crores has been granted. However, the said plan and the budget are not available in the public domain and have been denied under Sec. 8.1 (a) of the Right to Information Act (2005) by the MoEFCC. According to the minutes of the meeting of the project's monitoring committees held on 21 November 2024, which were made public recently, it was declared that SACON will receive Rs. 59.49 crores over thirty years. Rupees 12.66 crores have already been sanctioned for the first five years. SACON has sought two years to prepare a WCP after undertaking baseline studies, for which project positions have been recently advertised.

We posited our criticisms of the environmental impact assessment conducted by VIMTA, Hyderabad during the public hearing in January 2022, and offered a scientific projection of the endangerments. Amidst the ever-growing shreds of evidence in primatological research, and disconcerting revelations about the project, we firmly assert that no WCP is capable of mitigating the large-scale deforestation and land use alterations purported by the project due to the undermentioned reasons:

1. Nicobar long-tailed macaques exhibit an incapability to tolerate high temperature and humidity, perhaps due to the colour of their fur like other rainforest-adapted mammals. In Nicobar, the temperature difference between vegetated and de-vegetated spaces can vary from 0.3°C to over 1.5°C, and given

that it takes an average of 145 kilometres poleward migration or a 167 metre altitudinal shift in order to offset a temperature increase of 1°C, thermal vulnerabilities of macaques will compound by several fold. Clear felling of trees will contribute to spikes in local atmospheric temperature and humidity, and deregulate rainforest-driven thermal buffers. Added to this are contributors such as heatwaves and dry spells, both of which are projected to increase in the Nicobar region. Together they will create large expanses of permanently unsuitable spaces on the island. Attesting to these predictions, primates are increasingly dying of dehydration, heat stress and heatstroke even within degraded forests.

2. Together with the predicted loss of overall moisture from the island ecosystems due to climate change, massive deforestation will amplify the ongoing decline in precipitation. The sudden fall in precipitation will further diminish natural food resources and their diversity for the macaques and compel greater dependence on cultivars and anthropogenic sources, exacerbating existing hostilities with people such as poisoning, injuring, shooting, etc. This process is already in effect due to previous deforestation events.

Apart from the above unaccounted factors, there are likely to be other 'unknown' unknowns that will threaten the survival of the macaque. A land use change of such a massive scale will not only push the species towards functional extinction (i.e., where macaque's contributions to the ecosystem are lost) but also threaten floral and faunal species that are ecologically linked with it. Examples of the impact of large-scale deforestation on island-dwelling long-tailed macaques exist from Simeulue Island, Indonesia and Borneo. In the former case, population size is estimated to have declined by 99.5 per cent in forty years (retaliatory killing is an additional reason).

Additionally, the Nicobar long-tailed macaque is a remarkably understudied species, and it is impossible to gather critical data to inform its conservation and management in a short span of two years, the time sought by SACON to prepare a WCP. Some of this non-existent information includes but is not limited to the undermentioned:

1. Information on population density and population dynamics, i.e. the trend of birth and death rates of the sub-species, and how population parameters are impacted by burgeoning anthropogenic factors such as habitat loss, habitat degradation and climate change are absent. Despite macaques being conspicuous in urban areas, there is a high chance that the coastal population is declining.
2. The population genetic structures of Nicobar long-tailed macaques will offer insight into how genetically distinct or similar they are with each other. Genetic studies can also reveal the prevalence of alleles that might render them vulnerable to diseases or deformities/disabilities, the extent of thermal/humidity tolerance, the propensity for obesity due to a potential dependence on processed foods and more. This information will also offer clues on how macaques are responding to current anthropogenic adversities .
3. Information on the ecological role and relationships of the macaques with their habitats, other species, and broadly with the island ecosystem is unavailable. For instance, the macaque is anticipated to play functions critical to the ecosystem functioning of the island, such as indirectly regulating its climate, hydrology, even human food security through direct nutrient cycling, controlling agricultural insect pests, etc.

4. Ecological, behavioral, and sociocultural heterogeneities among macaque groups are unknown. Conservation sciences assume individuals and groups to be homogeneous beyond reason, and therefore apply findings from a small subset of animals to large heterogeneous populations, resulting in not only failed interventions but also irreversible impacts that are seldom documented. Groups differ in the foods they eat, in ways they form relationships, in ways they communicate through gestures, etc., and, therefore, such variations are inherent and critical to a species, and ought to be studied before developing a WCP.
5. Information on immunology and parasitic load of macaques is non-existent. Pathogens move among the species sharing close spaces. As these spaces or interfaces expand and agents alien to the island move in, they introduce novel sets of microbes. These microbes harm and decimate native biota. Therefore, it is essential to assess macaques' broad immunological vulnerabilities.

Without comprehensive long-term research on the unique features of the Nicobar long-tailed macaque on an island that is equally unique, and in absence of a 'proof of concept', a WCP risks straying from objectivity and practicality, reducing it to a hollow procedural exercise. But most crucially, what good is a WCP when instead of informing policies it is obligated to clean up its mess? Biodiversity conservation does not operate independent of other project decisions, and therefore an honest implementation of conservation action will invariably interfere with other project decisions. Therefore, the bigger question is, what is the weightage given to biodiversity while planning and executing mega-scale projects?

It is clear that this megaproject is indifferent towards the natural ecosystem, and if executed, will endanger an already 'vulnerable' macaque and gradually wreck its entire ecosystem. We restate our stand three years hence, and maintain that the Nicobar long-tailed macaque has been facing unprecedented threats in Great Nicobar, especially post-tsunami, and peri-urban groups are scrambling for survival and diminishing in population. The proposed project will directly impact about twenty-seven groups and expose the rest to severe vulnerabilities. As primatologists, we have witnessed similar scenarios play out repeatedly across the globe too often, and we are acutely aware of how they progress and conclude. We are bound by morality and ethics to state that we cannot be a party to the brutalities to be inflicted upon the island and the species thereof by remaining a mute spectator. We stand in absolute opposition to the Great Nicobar Project. Our solidarity also extends to the two indigenous communities, and we appeal for their rights, worldviews, and demands to be privileged over any other interests in every project decision. How is a project 'holistic' if it repeatedly undermines indigenous beings, humans and nonhumans? In the true interest of our nation, and fulfillment of our constitutional duties, we remind citizens that biodiversity is our collective heritage and pride, and therefore, it is our responsibility, and duty to pass it on to the next generation in their robust and functional states.

ANNEXURE 4
Brief Project Timeline

28 July 2020: The Andaman and Nicobar Islands Integrated Development Corporation (ANIIDCO) is designated the nodal agency for the implementation of the holistic development plan for Great Nicobar Island.

September 2020: NITI Aayog issues a 201-page request for proposal (RfP) for 'Preparation of Master Plan for Holistic Development of Great Nicobar Island'.

October 2020: Andaman and Nicobar Forest Department sends the proposal for the diversion of 121.87 square kilometres of forest land and 8.88 square kilometres of deemed forest for sustainable development in Great Nicobar (Phase-I) to the Ministry of Environment, Forest and Climate Change (MoEFCC).

January 2021: Galathea Bay Wildlife Sanctuary and Megapode Wildlife Sanctuary are de-notified.

March 2021: Publication by AECOM of a 126-page pre-feasibility report titled 'Holistic Development of Great Nicobar Island at Andaman and Nicobar Islands'.

5–6 April: 260th meeting of the EAC Infra-I: The Expert Appraisal Committee (EAC) recommended the Great Nicobar proposal for grant of Terms of Reference (ToR) for preparation of Environmental Impact Assistance (EIA)/Environmental Management Plan (EMP) report.

1 January 2022: Public hearing for the EIA study held at Campbell Bay.

6 March 2022: ANIIDCO submits the final EIA study and application for environmental and CRZ clearance to EAC Infra-I.

22–23 August 2022: 306th meeting of EAC Infra-I: EAC recommends the project for approval.

27 October 2022: Stage I in-principal forest clearance granted.

11 November 2022: Environmental clearance issued to the project proponent.

December 2022: Petitions filed in the National Green Tribunal (NGT) challenging the environmental, Coastal Regulation Zone (CRZ) and forest clearances granted to the project.

27 January 2023: Ministry of Ports, Shipping and Waterways invites expression of interest (EoI) for construction of port in Galathea Bay.

April 2023: Final hearing before a special five-member bench of the NGT, which sets up a high-powered committee to revisit certain aspects of the clearances.

18 April 2023: L&T Ltd., Afcons Infrastructure Ltd. and JSW Infrastructure Ltd. along with seven other domestic and global players respond to EoIs for building the ICTT.

21 May 2023: Reports of non-islanders not being issued ship tickets for travelling to Great Nicobar continue to emerge two months after the 'unofficial rule' was first exercised.

7 February 2024: Genocide scholars from thirteen countries write to the President regarding the impact on the Shompen community and urging to scrap the project.

4 March 2024: A total of 22,425 hectares of land spread across five districts of Haryana given protected forest status by the MoEFCC to make up for the loss of forest in Great Nicobar.

28 June 2024: The Central Information Commission of India upholds non-disclosure of information on forest diversion citing strategic nature of GNI project, only allows information on afforestation.

28 July 2024: The NGT appointed High-Powered Committee concludes that the proposed port site at Galathea Bay is not ICRZ-1A but ICRZ-1B.

28 August 2024: ANIIDCO invites EoI from interested parties for enumeration, felling, logging and transportation of trees for the township.

4 September 2024: Galathea Bay gets notifed as a major port.

15 September 2024: Notified Arravalli forest portion sold for mining.

17 December 2024: RTI response reveals Ministry of Ports, Shipping and Waterways has sought 100 acres of seafront land in GNI for ship building and repair facility, an export-import port at Campbell Bay and a cruise terminal at Galathea Bay.

18 December 2024: A petition filed in Calcutta High Court challenging the violations of the Forest Rights Act in granting the clearances to the mega infrastructure project.

1 January 2025: The Town and Country Planning Unit, Andaman and Nicobar Administration issues a letter for obtaining the views of the Gram Panchayats for notifying the project area as 'Great Nicobar Island Development Area' under the Andaman and Nicobar Town and Country Planning Regulation, 1994.

4 February 2025: Shipping Minister says that Ministry of Ports, Shipping and Waterways has has requested MHA to allocate appropriate space in the master plan for developing an international and domestic cruise ship in Great Nicobar Island.

21 February 2025: Calcutta High Court directs the MoEFCC to respond to the 2021 notification declaring 0 kilometre eco-sensitive zones (ESZ) around the Galathea National and Campbell Bay National Park.

12 March 2025: Minister for Tribal Affairs denies receiving any objections from the tribal communities or anthropologists and activists regarding the impact of the Great Nicobar project.

11 April 2025: Directorate of Social Welfare, Andaman and Nicobar issues a notification for conducting Social Impact Assessment for the acquisition of 666.44 hectares land for construction of road infrastructure.

Detailed timeline:

To access a detailed timeline of the project and relevant documents, scan the QR

Notes

Editor's Note: Closer to the Precipice

1. See 'Insights into Tectonic Hazards Since the 2004 Indian Ocean Earthquake and Tsunami', *Nature Reviews Earth and Environment*, December 2024, https://tinyurl.com/3asanzet.
2. https://tinyurl.com/yse52xr8.
3. Different stories in this collection quote different figures. We have retained the original figures to reflect these changes that have taken place in such a short time.

1. An Island on Edge

1. Trunk infrastructure refers to primary, shared infrastructure systems.
2. AECOM India Pvt Ltd, 'Holistic Development of Great Nicobar Island of Andaman & Nicobar Islands: Pre-Feasibility Report', AECOM India Pvt Ltd, 2021.
3. ANIIDCO, 'Expression of Interest for Enumeration, Felling, Logging and Transportation of Trees for Holistic Development of Great Nicobar Island Project', Ref No: F.No: 1-1586/ANIIDCO/Projects/2021-22/Vol.IV/1732, ANIIDCO, 2024.
4. ANIIDCO, 'Minutes of meeting held at 4.00 pm on 04.10.2024 under the chairmanship of MD, ANIIDCO regarding review of issues related to Great Nicobar Island Project, ANIIDCO, Port Blair, October 2024.

5   See https://www.bnhs.org/public/hornbill_pdf/HORNBILL_ J-S%202018_red.pdf.

9. 20 Christmases After the Tsunami

1   All names have been changed to protect the identity of the individuals.

11. An Obit for Patai Takaru

1   See, for instance, https://www.theatlantic.com/science/archive/2017/12/trofim-lysenko-soviet-union-russia/54878; R. Lewontin, and R. Levins, 'The Problem of Lysenkoism', in H. Rose and S. Rose (eds), *The Radicalisation of Science*, Critical Social Studies (Palgrave, London, 1976).
2   P. Sekhsaria, *The Great Nicobar Betrayal* (THG Publishing Private Limited, Chennai, 2024). [Articles compiled in this publication present critiques on various aspects.]; N. Moorthy, 'Great Nicobar Port Project: The Red Flags in EIA Report That Have Gone Ignored', *The Quint*, 19 September 2024, https://www.thequint.com/opinion/central-government-great-nicobar-island-port-project-flaws-red-flags-i a-report-ignored.
3   A. Dhillon, 'India's Plan for Untouched Nicobar Isles Will Be "Death Sentence" for Isolated Tribe', *The Guardian*, 7 February 2024, https://www.theguardian.com/global-development/2024/feb/07/india-port-airport-power-plant-military-project-great-nicobar-island-death-sentence-shompen-indigenous-people-warning; R. Pardikar, 'Nicobarese Anthropologist & Former Officer Questions Modi Govt Claims O Controversial Great Nicobar Project'. *Article-14*, 30 September 2024, https://article-14.com/post/nicobarese-anthropologist-former-officer-questions-modi-govt-claims-over-cooversial-great-nicobar-project-66f9d6522240e.
4   S. Ganapathi, 'A "Major Port" in Great Nicobar Island: A Byproduct of "Make in India" Syndrome?' *The Quint*, 7 September 2024, https://www.thequint.com/opinion/great-nicobar-island-major-port-environmental-damage-unviable-transshipment-project; Civil Society, 'Goodbye to the Great Nicobar?' *Civil Society*, 28 September 2024, https://www.civilsocietyonline.com/cover-story/goodbye-to-the-great-nicobar/.
5   Civil Society, 'Possible to Bolster Security Without Harming Ecology'. *Civil Society*, 28 September 2024, https://www.

civilsocietyonline.com/cover-add-ons/possible-to-bolster-security-without-harming-ecology/.

6. G. Umapathy, M. Singh and S.M. Mohnot, 'Status and Distribution of *Macaca fascicularis umbrosa in the Nicobar Islands*, India', *International Journal of Primatology*, vol. 24, 2003, pp. 281–93. The paper reported a density of 997 trees per hectare of stems greater than 15 cm girth at breast height (GBH). Even conservatively considering a density of 600 trees per hectare with stems >30 cm GBH and a forest destruction area of 6599 ha suggests nearly 40 lakh trees will be destroyed.

7. See Vaishnavi Rathore, '1 Crore Trees—Not 8.5 Lakh—Could Be Cut for Great Nicobar Project, One Ecologist Estimates', *Scroll.in*, 10 October 2024, https://scroll.in/article/1074221/1-crore-trees-not-8-5-lakh-could-be-cut-for-great-nicobar-project-one-ecologist-estimates.

8. The details are not available in the EIA, although some figures appear to be presented in a blurry and unreadable form in an Annexure X.

9. V. Rathore, 'Can a Safari Park Outside Delhi Make Up for a Lost Nicobar Forest?' *Scroll.in*, 19 April 2023, https://scroll.in/article/1047526/can-a-safari-park-outside-delhi-make-up-for-a-lost-nicobar-forest.

10. CAG, Report of the Controller and Auditor General of India on Compensatory Afforestation in India, compliance audit, No. 21 of 2013, New Delhi.

11. M. Arasumani, D. Khan, C.K. Vishnudas, M. Muthukumar, M. Bunyan and V.V. Robin, 2019, 'Invasion Compounds an Ecosystem-wide Loss to Afforestation in the Tropical Grasslands of the Shola Sky Islands', *Biological Conservation*, vol. 230, pp. 141–50; M. Asher and P. Bhandari, 'Mitigation or Myth? Impacts of Hydropower Development and Compensatory Afforestation on Forest Ecosystems in the High Himalayas', *Land Use Policy*, vol. 100, 2021, p. 105041; E.A. Coleman, B. Schultz, V. Ramprasad, H. Fischer, P. Rana, A.M. Filippi and F. Fleischman, 'Limited Effects of Tree Planting on Forest Canopy Cover and Rural Livelihoods in Northern India', *Nature Sustainability*, vol. 4, 2021, pp. 997–1004; P. Rana, F. Fleischman, V. Ramprasad and K. Lee, 'Predicting Wasteful Spending in Tree Planting Programs in Indian Himalaya', World Development, vol. 154, p. 105864; S. Tambe, G.S. Rawat, P. Krishen, M.K. Ranjitsinh, N. Ghosh, A.S. Rawat and J. Takpa, 2022. 'Compensatory Afforestation Policy in India: An Analysis Using an Ecorestoration Lens', *International Forestry Review*, vol. 24, no. 4, 2022, pp. 607–18.

12. A. Di Sacco, K.A. Hardwick, D. Blakesley, P.H.S. Brancalion, E. Breman, L. Cecilio Rebola, S. Chomba, K. Dixon, S. Elliott, G.

Ruyonga, K. Shaw, P. Smith, R.J. Smith, AND A. Antonelli, (2021), 'Ten Golden Rules for Reforestation to Optimize Carbon Sequestration, Biodiversity Recovery and Livelihood Benefits', Global Change Biology, vol. 27, pp. 1328–48, https://doi.org/10.1111/gcb.15498.

13 A. Rajpurohit (2023), 'SC-appointed Panel Warns Against Andaman's Proposal to 'Revive' Palm Oil Plantations', *Newslaundry*, 23 January 2023, https://www.newslaundry.com/2023/01/23/sc-appointed-panelwarns-against-andamans-proposal-to-revive palm-oil-plantations.

14 S. Sandilyan, B. Meenakumari, A. Biju Kumar, and Karthikeyan Vasudevan. (2018), *Impacts of Invasive Alien Species on Island Ecosystems of India with Special Reference to Andaman Group of Islands,* National Biodiversity Authority, Chennai.

15 A. Krishnan and A.M. Osuri (2023), 'Beyond the Passive–Active Dichotomy: Aligning Research with the Intervention Continuum Framework of Ecological Restoration', *Restoration Ecology*, vol. 31, p. e13828; Tambe et al. (2022), op. cit.

16 R. Crouzeilles et al. (2017), 'Ecological Restoration Success Is Higher for Natural Regeneration than for Active Restoration in Tropical Forests', *Science Advances*, vol. 3, p. e1701345; R.L. Chazdon and M. Uriarte (2016), 'Natural Regeneration in the Context of Large-scale Forest and Landscape Restoration in the Tropics', Biotropica, vol. 48, pp. 709–15.

17 A.M. Osuri, S. Kasinathan, M.K. Siddhartha, D. Mudappa and T.R.S. Raman (2019), 'Effects of Restoration on Tree Communities and Carbon Storage in Rainforest Fragments of the Western Ghats, India', *Ecosphere*, vol.10, no. 9, p. e02860.

18 Osuri et al. (2019), op. cit.

19 Di Sacco et al. (2021), op. cit.

20 Lisa Boström-Einarsson, Russell C. Babcock, Elisa Bayraktarov, Daniela Ceccarelli, Nathan Cook, Sebastian C.A. Ferse, Boze Hancock et al. (2020), 'Coral Restoration: A Systematic Review of Current Methods, Successes, Failures and Future Directions', PloS One, vol. 15, p. e0226631.

21 Reported in Vimta and ANIIDCO (2022), Anticipated Environmental Impacts and Mitigation Measures; in *Comprehensive Environmental Impact Assessment Report*, Chapter 4A: C4-C11.

22 Terry P. Hughes, Andrew H. Baird, Tiffany H. Morrison and Gergely Torda (2023), 'Principles for Coral Reef Restoration in the Anthropocene', *One Earth*, vol. 6, pp. 656–65.

23 Robert P. Streit, Tiffany H. Morrison and David R. Bellwood (2024), 'Coral Reefs Deserve Evidence-based Management Not Heroic Interference', *Nature Climate Change*, vol. 14, pp. 773–75.

24 T.R. McClanahan, E.S. Darling, J.M. Maina, N.A. Muthiga, Stephanie D'agata, S.D. Jupiter, R. Arthur, S.K. Wilson, S. Mangubhai, Y. Nand, A.M. Ussi, A.T. Humphries, V.J. Patankar, M.M.M. Guillaume, S.A. Keith, G. Shedrawi, P. Julius, G. Grimsditch, J. Ndagala and J. Leblond (2019), 'Temperature Patterns and Mechanisms Influencing Coral Bleaching During the 2016 El Niño', *Nature Climate Change*, vol. 9, p. 845.

13. Questioning Government Claims

1   Run by the Andaman and Nicobar administration's department of tribal welfare, the AAJVS addresses issues related to the welfare of particularly vulnerable tribal groups, such as the Shompen.
2   The Andaman Trunk Road gave settlers and tourists unfettered access to areas reserved for the Jarawa tribe, sparking a number of problems, such as exploitation, exposure to diseases, logging, poaching and encroachment of forests.

16. A Port of No Return

1   This article is a re-written version based on two short editorial pieces 'A Port of No Return', *Indian Express*, 14 August 2024 and 'In Nicobar Ecology Loses Out, but Who Receives a Windfall?' *Hindustan Times*, 11 March 2025.

About the Contributors

Ajay Saini is an anthropologist with extensive research experience in the Andaman and Nicobar Islands. He teaches at the Indian Institute of Technology, Delhi.

Anvita Abbi is a distinguished scholar of minority languages. She worked with the last speakers of the Great Andamanese language family and taught linguistics at Jawaharlal Nehru University.

M. Rajshekhar is an independent reporter who writes on environment, development and India's steady slide into authoritarianism. He is also the author of *Despite the State: Why India Lets Its People Down and How They Cope*, a book on the eroding social contract between Indians and the country's political parties.

Leesha K. Nair is a freelance journalist from the Andaman and Nicobar Islands, focusing on intersecting themes of gender, environment, climate, mental health and indigenous issues. Her work has been featured in publications such as *The Diplomat, The Hindu, AAJA-Asia, Maktoob Media and Core Middle East*, among others.

Manish Chandi has worked in the Andaman and Nicobar Islands on the interface between communities and nature for twenty-four years. His interests and work have included surveys and research work on saltwater crocodiles, sea turtles, forest trees and indigenous communities.

Pankaj Sekhsaria has worked on issues of the Andaman and Nicobar Islands for over three decades. He has authored/edited seven books on the islands, including *The Last Wave: An Island Novel, Waiting for Turtles* and *The Great Nicobar Betrayal*.

Rishika Pardikar is a freelance environment and climate reporter based in Bangalore. She covers science, law and policy.

Rohan Arthur is a marine scientist who works on climate change impacts on nearshore marine ecosystems, and is concerned with issues of human survival and well-being on low-lying coral atolls. He works in the oceanic islands of India and along its coasts.

Saurav Harikumar is a wildlife biologist, conservationist and author. He is currently based in Brisbane, Australia, where he is working on getting his PhD in mammalian niche ecology.

Suman S. has worked in the Andaman and Nicobar Islands for many years. Their identity has been concealed to protect their ability to continue working here in the future.

Tansy Troy is an India-based writer, illustrator, poet and educator. She edits young people's eco journal *The Apple Press* and publishes regularly in *Scroll.in* and *The Chakkar*. She also reviews and writes articles, interviews and poems for *Frontline, Sanctuary Asia, Open Magazine, HT, The Hindu, Punch Magazine, Usawa* and *Art Amour*.

T.R. Shankar Raman is a writer and wildlife scientist who studies the ecology and conservation of tropical forests and wildlife. He lives and works in the Anaimalai Hills. He's the author of *The Wild*

Heart of India and blogs at View from Elephant Hills https://shankarraman.in.

Vaishnavi Rathore is a climate and land reporter with *Scroll.in* and covers stories on climate justice, environmental degradation, climate change, politics of land, rivers and forests. She reports extensively from ground across the country and her work has won multiple awards.